JoJo's Guide TO

BY JoJo Siwa

Making Your Own Fun

#DOITYOURSELF

Amulet Books
New York

Library of Congress Cataloging-in-Publication Data
Names: Siwa, JoJo, 2003– author.
Title: JoJo's guide to making your own fun: #doityourself / by JoJo Siwa.
Description: New York: Amulet Books, 2018.
Identifiers: LCCN 2018001106 | ISBN 9781419732089 (hardcover pob)
Subjects: LCSH: Amusements—Juvenile literature. | Handicraft—Juvenile literature. | Creative activities and
seat work—Juvenile literature. | Conduct of life—Juvenile literature. | Siwa, JoJo, 2003—Juvenile literature.
Classification: LCC GV1203 .S545 2018 | DDC 793—dc23

ISBN 978-1-4197-3208-9

Jacket illustrations copyright © 2018 Siobhán Gallagher
Book design by Caitlin Keegan

Printed and bound in U.S.A.
10 9 8 7 6 5 4 3 2 1

ABRAMS The Art of Books
195 Broadway, New York, NY 10007
abramsbooks.com

Activities

· ·

Fall

(September–November)

1

Fall Word Scramble

Who doesn't love fall? It's time for going back to school, layering sweaters and scarves, raking leaves, and giving thanks. Let's kick off the season with a few of our favorite fall words!

Can you unscramble these fall words?

CLOOSH ______________________

VESHTAR ______________________

WEENOAHLL ______________________

LPPAES ______________________

PKINSMUP ______________________

KSTHNIAVIGGN ______________________

Answers: school, harvest, Halloween, apples, pumpkins, Thanksgiving

New teachers!
New lessons!
New friends!

Get Ready for the First Day of School!

It's not unusual to get a case of the back-to-school jitters as fall begins. Sometimes, the best way to combat the jitters is to make sure you're prepared. Here are a few ideas that can help you (and your parents) get ready for the first day of school.

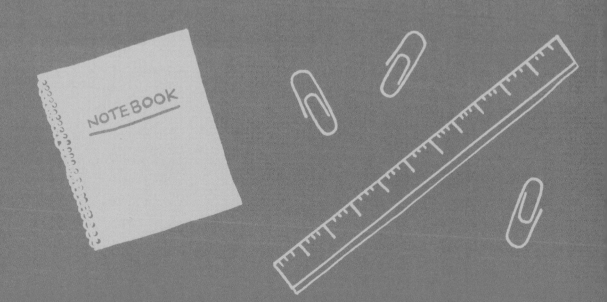

NOTEBOOK

Idea #1: Pick out a special outfit.

Have you ever noticed how you always feel a little bit better when you love what you're wearing? Take JoJo and her signature accessory—a big bow. You're just more confident when you love your outfit. Plus, it's your chance to tell the world something about yourself without saying a word. So pair your favorite skirt with a special T-shirt, or pick out your own signature accessory—a bow like JoJo's (more on that later!), a stack of your favorite bracelets, or maybe a necklace that used to belong to your mom. Whatever you're wearing, make sure it *feels* right. Try to find an outfit that really says "This is me!"

Combat the back-to-school jitters!

Idea #2: Buy school supplies.

JoJo and her mom love going to the homeschooling store in Nebraska. Sometimes, having just the right tool makes learning even more fun. If math isn't your favorite subject, maybe you'll like it a little bit better if you have a special pencil that you use specifically for math lessons. Or maybe reading isn't your thing, but a special bookmark makes you smile every time you open a book. Be creative! Shopping for school supplies is a lot of fun, and with the right pencils, pens, and notebooks, you'll be prepared for whatever your teacher throws your way!

Idea #3: Set up a schedule.

Maybe scheduling your time doesn't sound like the most exciting or glamorous thing in the world, but how else are you going to get everything done? JoJo has to balance school, dancing, and singing—just to name a few things!—and without a schedule, it would be tough to find the time to fit everything in. So sit down with your parents before the first day of school and make a list of all the things you want to do this year: Maybe you want to take piano lessons after school, try out for the softball team, or leave an hour at the end of the day for playing on the computer. And if your mom is worried that all these activities won't leave enough time for homework, you can build time into your schedule for that too! (But always leave a little free time in case something unexpected comes up!)

Got any more ideas for back-to-school prep? Add them here!

_____

_____

_____

_____

_____

_____

_____

_____

_____

_____

_____

_____

JOJO FACTS

- School is one of JoJo's favorite things!

- Homeschooling was the right fit for JoJo from the start—she was proactive about learning and was juggling the crazy hours that came with her love of dance.

- JoJo already knew how to read by the time she went to kindergarten!

JoJo is a big believer in practice and preparation!

Work hard!

3

GOALS FOR THE SCHOOL YEAR—AND BEYOND

There's one thing JoJo loves every bit as much as she loves school—setting goals! Whether your goal is to be an international singing sensation or to get a perfect score on your social studies test, you have to give your best effort to achieve your dreams! JoJo has a million goals, but she has a plan to achieve each of them. You should too!

Some Sample Goals

Goal #1: Be polite to your teacher.

It sounds simple, but it makes a big difference! Learning new things is exciting, but trying to understand something for the first time can also be frustrating. A good attitude—good manners, a big smile—can go a long way.

Goal #2: Make new friends.

Be a little (or a lot!) different!

Maybe you're in a new classroom this year, and your best friends from last year are in a different one. Instead of being bummed that your friends aren't with you every day, think of this as an opportunity to make new friends! You can still see your old friends after school, right? Or maybe you and your best friends are lucky enough to be in the same class for another year. That doesn't mean you can't invite a new friend to join your squad!

Goal #3: Work hard.

Like JoJo says, once you've achieved one tough goal, you'll know anything is possible! But you have to be willing to work hard to get there. JoJo had to learn the tech skills to edit her YouTube videos *and* find the time to schedule dance every day. Hard work is the key to following your dreams!

MESSAGE FROM JOJO

"Find the thing that you love and go after it, Siwanatorz! Hard work is the absolute opposite of boring if you have a passion."

JOJO FACTS

- JoJo's goal has always been to be someone *big*.

- JoJo decided long ago that one of her goals was to be a pop star, and she's on her way to becoming one!

What are your goals—for school this year and for the rest of your life? It's never too early to start planning!

_____

_____

_____

_____

_____

_____

_____

_____

_____

_____

_____

_____

_____

Embrace your inner nerd!

First Day of School?
Put Yourself Out There!

Okay, so it's the first day of school. You're wearing your special outfit, and you and your parents have planned your schedule. But maybe you haven't met your new teacher, or you're starting at a new school and haven't made any friends yet. Putting yourself out there is how you show people who you are. Here are a few tips to help you get started!

A good first impression is key!

JOJO FACTS

- JoJo has to walk into new situations all the time: auditions, business meetings, dance classes, etc. You know how she handles it? By *putting herself out there.*

- JoJo meets lots of new people—really successful people like producers, casting directors, and executives. You know how she handles it? By *putting herself out there.*

Some Tips for Putting Yourself Out There

Tip #1: Introduce yourself!
Go up to your new teacher and say, "Hi, I'm [fill in the blank] and I'm so excited to be joining your classroom this year!" Trust us, your teacher will probably think, "This kid introduced him/herself. He/She was really nice."

Tip #2: Meet new people!
See someone you want to be friends with? Maybe you like her hairstyle or her T-shirt, or there's something about her that just looks *right?* Tell her! Go right on up to her, tap her on the back, and say, "Hi, I'm [fill in the blank] and I love your [fill in the blank]." After you introduce yourself and say hello, it's weird—it's like you're friends already.

Tip #3: Find common traits!
What if you see someone who looks just as nervous as you are? Maybe you're not the only new kid in the class, or maybe you have a classmate who's pretty shy. Now's your chance to help someone else open up!
Go up to them and say, "Hi, I'm [fill in the blank] and I noticed you seem kind of shy. Want to be shy together?" Sometimes people seem standoffish and intimidating when they're really just quiet and nervous.

Tell people how happy you are to meet them!

Tip #4: Show off your personality!

Remember when we talked about picking out an outfit for the first day of school? That's also part of putting yourself out there! When JoJo wears her bow, it's her way of telling total strangers something about herself. Find the right accessory to tell the world something about yourself! Love books? Carry around your favorite so that you can recommend it to your new friends. Love softball? How about wearing a ball-shaped charm on a necklace or bracelet? Love your dog? Carry around a picture so you can show off his cuteness any time the subject comes up!

Put yourself out there!

13

5

Decorate Socks—
One Pair for You and One for
One of Your New Friends!

One way to express yourself is to design and decorate your clothing yourself! Start small, like decorating a pair of socks.

Sock Time!

Step #1

Make sure you have a parent's permission. You can revamp an old pair of socks, or get a new pair just for decorating.

Step #2

You'll need some supplies. Puff paint is a great option! Also, you can use stick-on sequins, fabric markers, and glitter glue.

Step #3

Go crazy! Express yourself! Love reading? Draw a book on the side of your socks with a fabric marker. Love to shine? Cover those socks with more glitter glue than previously thought possible. Love pink? Paint them pink!

Step #4

Don't stop at just one pair of socks for yourself. Decorate a pair for a friend too! You can design a pair to represent your friend's personality or to represent your personality so your friend will always think of you when wearing them!

Siwanatorz aren't afraid to be a little different!

Be your wacky, wonderful self on the inside and the outside.

MESSAGE FROM JOJO

"If everyone else is wearing sweatpants, wear sequins!"

Grandparents are the best!

6

Celebrate Grandparents Day!

Grandparents Day is a great excuse to tell your grandparents just how much they mean to you.

~~JOJO~~ JAYDEN FACTS
. . . .

- JoJo's brother, Jayden, was always really close to their grandmother—they used to hang out so much that JoJo thinks some of Grandma's personality rubbed off on Jayden!

- Their grandmother loved to cook, so Jayden loves to cook too.

- Jayden is a master at what JoJo calls the Grandma Rule. It says that if you wouldn't say it or do it around your grandma, don't say or do it at all!

Unfortunately, some of us don't have our grandparents with us anymore. But that doesn't mean we can't find a way to celebrate Grandparents Day. Maybe there's someone in your life who's like a grandparent to you. Telling them so will definitely brighten their day. Or maybe you lost a grandparent recently. You can use Grandparents Day as a time to reflect on all the lessons your grandparents taught you during their lives.

What is a lesson you learned from a grandparent?

_____

_____

_____

_____

_____

_____

_____

MESSAGE FROM JOJO
"Follow the Grandma Rule!"

JoJo's Grandma's Banana Muffins

Ingredients:

- 5 tablespoons butter
- 3 ripe bananas
- ¾ cup sugar
- 1½ cups flour
- 1 teaspoon baking soda
- 1 teaspoon baking powder
- 1 egg

Directions:
1. With an adult's help, preheat oven to 350 degrees.
2. Melt butter in the microwave using a microwave-safe bowl.
3. While butter is melting, mash the bananas in a small bowl and set aside.
4. Combine sugar, flour, baking soda, and baking powder in a medium-sized bowl.
5. Add melted butter to the bananas and beat in the egg.
6. Pour the banana mixture into the dry ingredients; mix with a spoon until batter is smooth.
7. Pour batter evenly into a 12-muffin pan lined with paper baking cups, leaving ½ inch of space from the top of each cup for the batter to rise.
8. Bake for 20–30 minutes, or until muffins are golden brown and a toothpick inserted into the center of a muffin comes out clean.
9. Enjoy!

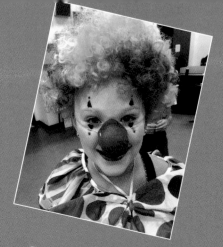

7

DON'T WAIT FOR HALLOWEEN TO DRESS UP—BE YOURSELF EVERY DAY! (AND IF ALL ELSE FAILS, THROW A COSTUME PARTY!)

JoJo loves dressing up. Maybe you're not a performer like JoJo, so you don't get to dress up all the time. But that doesn't mean you can't express yourself every day. And if you still need an excuse to dress up, throw a costume party!

JoJo's Tips for Throwing the World's Greatest Costume Party

Tip #1: Pick a theme.

On Halloween, anything goes. People dress up as cats and witches, wizards and monkeys, and that's pretty awesome. Who doesn't like a day when everyone can be anything they want to be? But you can make your party a little more specific by picking a theme for everyone's costumes: Tell your friends to dress as their favorite superhero or as a character from your favorite movie or fairy tale. Or ask everyone to have at least one pink item in their costume (or whatever your favorite color may be), or even ask them to wear a JoJo-style bow in their hair!

Tip #2: Invite everyone.

Okay, not actually *everyone*—your house probably can't fit that many people. But invite generously! Is there a kid in your class who sort of intimidates you? Well, here's your excuse to finally talk to them. Is there another kid who's been getting picked on by the class bully? Invite that person too—you'll probably make their day! How about your grandma? Or your teacher? The more the merrier! (Just make sure it's okay with your mom and dad!)

Tip #3: Go all out.

As the host, it's your job to set an example in the costume department. So think big! Does your costume call for glitter? Use all the glitter! Would your costume be a little cooler if you took the time to curl your hair? Then curl your hair! Do whatever it takes to make your costume amazing.

Everyone loves a good costume!

JOJO FACTS

....

- JoJo loved her first costume so much that she would have slept in it if she could!

- JoJo's first dance costume featured—you guessed it—bows! It wasn't long before bows became JoJo's signature accessory!

Tip #4: Share the love.

Not everyone loves dressing up. In fact, for some people, it might feel more like work than fun. So make sure your guests know how much you appreciate the effort they put into dressing up. After all, they're doing it for *your* party! Compliment their costumes, even if they're not nearly as elaborate as yours.

MESSAGE FROM JOJO

"What's one of the best things about being a dancer? You don't have to wait for Halloween to wear costumes!"

8

Slimy!

Make Homemade Slime

There's more to Halloween than costumes and candy. There are also ghosts, ghouls, haunted houses, and the chance to gross out your friends with a practical joke or two. Slime can come in handy when it's time for jokes and gross-outs. Plus, you can make it with your friends!

Ew!

Before you get started, make sure you have a grown-up's permission. This can get kind of messy!

Ingredients:

- 4 ounces school glue
- ½ tablespoon baking soda
- Food coloring
- 1 tablespoon contact lens solution, plus a little extra (make sure you get the kind that contains boric acid)

JOJO FACT

- JoJo loves a good practical joke!

Gross!

Step #1: Pour the school glue into a small bowl.

Step #2: Mix in the baking soda. For stretchier slime, add some water.

Step #3: Add food coloring until the slime is exactly the right color.

Ick!

Step #4: Add the contact lens solution.

Step #5: Keep mixing! Slime will begin to form. Take the slime out of the bowl and knead it like dough. Too sticky? Add more contact lens solution. Keep kneading until it feels like slime.

Bonus Step: Want to take your slime to the next level? Add glitter along with the food coloring!

25

9

Decorate Homemade
Caramel Apples

Fall is apple time—apple pies, apple cider donuts,
apple fritters, and, of course, caramel apples!
Sure, you can buy them already made, but it's
way more fun to decorate them yourself.

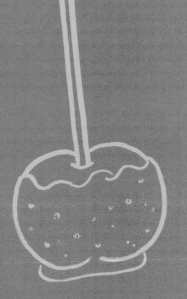

Delicious!

A Step-by-Step Guide to Caramel Apple Domination

Step #1: Buy your favorite apples.
There are so many different kinds of apples! Macintosh, Gala, Honeycrisp, Red Delicious . . . What's your favorite?

Step #2: Buy some caramel.
This time of year, a lot of grocery stores have ready-made liquid caramel. Or you can buy pieces of caramel candy to melt.

Step #3: Stock up on toppings.
There are so many things that look and taste great on caramel apples! Mini chocolate chips. Sprinkles. Chopped nuts. Marshmallows. Crumbled-up cookies! You get the idea. Go nuts! (Ooh, nuts!)

Step #4: Prepare the apples.
Wash and dry your apples. Insert a popsicle stick where the stem sticks out. (Ask a grown-up to poke a hole in the apple with a knife first to make the sticks go in more easily.)

Step #5: Prepare the caramel.
If you bought liquid caramel, you're all set. If you need to melt your caramel, now's the time do it. (With help from a grown-up!) To melt caramel candy in a bowl, add a little bit of water to your caramel bits and zap them in the microwave until the caramel is melty and smooth.

Step #6: Dip the apples in the caramel!
Using the stick like a handle, dip your apples into the caramel. You can also use a spoon to spread the caramel on the outside of the apple if that works better for you.

Did you know that fall is famous for the fruits and vegetables that get harvested at this time of year?

Step #7: Roll the apples into your toppings.

Using the stick like a handle, roll your apples into your toppings. Or you can use a spoon (or your hand!) to stick the toppings to the caramel.

Step #8: Refrigerate the apples.

Stand the apples with sticks up on a tray, and place into your fridge until the caramel hardens.

Step #9: Eat and enjoy!

This step doesn't need much explaining.

10

Make Your Own Haunted House

Halloween is a great time to take your jokes to the next level. Invite your friends over, only to surprise them with the world's greatest homemade haunted house! Here are some tips to create the ultimate haunted house to freak out your friends.

Let's get haunted!

Tip #1: Make a Halloween wreath for your front door.

We're all used to seeing wreaths on doors in December, but how about a creepy Halloween wreath? Use a foam wreath form (you can find one at a crafts store), and glue all sorts of stuff to it! You can use mini pumpkins or stretch cotton balls into fake spiderwebs. Have some old dolls lying around? Take them apart and paste the parts to the form. They will look like creepy body parts!

Tip #2: Don't make it too easy to come inside.

Try hanging a row of scarves or a sheet across your front door so that people have to push it out of the way to come inside. Want to take it to the next level? Ask a parent or sibling to stand to one side and make scary noises as your friends are pushing the sheet or scarves aside. It's sure to give them a real fright!

Chills!

Tip #3: Create a mad scientist's lab.

Turn your kitchen into a creepy science lab! Ask your guests to put on blindfolds before stepping inside. Then, offer them bowls of food to touch—but not just any food! Offer them a bowl of peeled grapes and tell them they are eyeballs. Or a bowl of oily spaghetti that feels like guts or worms. And mushy cooked cauliflower can feel like a brain! Ewwww!!!

Thrills!

Tip #4: Turn your backyard into a spooky graveyard.

Use empty cereal boxes to design tombstones. Paint them black and gray, and put strange names on them like "Dr. Frankenstein" and "Mr. Hyde." If you want rounded tombstones, cut the top corners of the boxes with scissors to make a smooth, circular edge.

Frights!

Tip #5: Set the mood with some music.

Create a special playlist for your haunted house, complete with scary music and sound effects of glass breaking, someone screaming, and ghosts moaning. The right background music will help create a spooky atmosphere!

Tip #6: But don't make it too scary.

Halloween isn't only about scaring your friends. It's also about something more important—candy! So after you've forced your friends to walk through a scientist's lab and a creepy graveyard, lead them to bowls full of your favorite candy, with your favorite (non-spooky) music playing. Have fun!

JOJO FACT
....

- When JoJo was eight years old, she went to a haunted house with her dad in Omaha, Nebraska. It was scary—but so much fun!

MESSAGE FROM JOJO

"I like to mess with people (in a nice way)."

Spread the love!

11

DON'T JUST DRESS UP FOR HALLOWEEN THIS YEAR—DO SOME GOOD!

Halloween is also a chance to visit each of your neighbors and suggest something other than a trick or a treat. It can be a great opportunity to collect donations for a charity that's important to you. Create a special container to collect your donations in. Decorate it with the name of your charity and some words and pictures about why that charity means so much to you.

Make Your Own Collection Container

Option #1: Find a bucket.

Do you have any buckets left over from playing at the beach last summer? Dig them out of the back of your closet and get to work! First, decorate some sheets of paper with the name of your charity and a few words or images that explain why it means so much to you. Then glue or tape the pages around the bucket until it's completely covered. Collecting donations for an animal shelter? Cover your bucket with pictures of dogs and cats. Collecting donations for your local library? Cover your bucket with pictures of your favorite books.

Option #2: Repurpose a tote bag.

Maybe your mom has a spare plain tote bag you can use. (If not, you can usually find a plain bag at your local crafts store.) Use some fabric markers to draw directly onto the bag!

Do some good!

Not sure where to start? Here are some ideas!

- Raise money for your local animal shelter or hospital.

- Collect funds for natural-disaster relief efforts or for needy children around the world with an organization like UNICEF.

- There are so many worthy causes out there. Find one that's important to you, and spread the word!

Option #3: Decorate a pumpkin bucket.

You know those plastic pumpkin buckets you see everywhere this time of year? Buy one of those, then make it your own! Spray-paint it a completely different color. Use puff paint to write the name of your charity and your reasons for picking the charity. Even though you're collecting charitable donations, you're still celebrating Halloween. Repurposing a pumpkin bucket is a great way to do both at the same time!

MESSAGE FROM JOJO

"Give the kindness you want to receive."

12

Give Thanks

Thanksgiving is a pretty amazing holiday. Time off from school, turkey, pie, a house full of family and friends—it doesn't get much better. (Plus winter vacation is just around the corner!) But with all that good stuff, sometimes it's easy to lose sight of the real meaning behind the holiday. Thanksgiving is about food and family and friends, but it's also about giving thanks.

So this year, set aside some time on Thanksgiving to say thank you to the ones you love or, better yet, write thank-you notes to the people who help you have a #LuckyCharmedLife just like JoJo.

Say thank you . . .

You can thank people any way you want—in person, with a text message, with a post on social media or over email. But we think there's something special about handwritten thank-you notes. So pick up your favorite pen and start writing! Decorate the envelopes with stickers and glitter to make them really special!

. . . *to your teacher.*

Teachers work really hard, and students sometimes forget to say thank you. Maybe your favorite teacher stayed late one day after school to help you master a math concept that had been tripping you up. Or maybe a lesson from a teacher you had a few years ago has really stayed with you. Tell them how much their help meant to you.

. . . *to your mom.*

Let's face it: Moms are the best! JoJo's mom is her best friend, and JoJo never misses a chance to tell her mom how much she means to her. Take a few minutes on Thanksgiving to thank your mom for everything she does. (And thank Dad too!)

. . . *to your sibling—or someone who is like a sibling to you.*

Okay, so maybe you and your big brother don't always get along. Or maybe your little sister is constantly copying everything you do. But at the end of the day, our siblings know us in a way that nobody else ever will. And that's definitely worth a great big thank-you (at least) once a year!

. . . *to your best friends.*

There's a reason we call them our best friends. Tell them how lucky you are to have them or how glad you are that you all ended up in the same classroom or on the same softball team or in the same dance class. Whatever it was that brought you guys together, be grateful that you found your way to one another!

Who and what else are you thankful for?

Xièxiè!

13

MAKE YOUR OWN BOW—JUST LIKE JOJO!

If you're reading this book, then you probably already know that a bow is JoJo's signature accessory. Show the world that you're a Siwanator with your very own bow.

Show the world you're a Siwanator!

Make a bow in six simple steps!

You'll need ribbon and an elastic hair tie. The longer your ribbon, the bigger your bow will be!

Step #1: Pull the ribbon through the elastic hair tie so that there are equal lengths of ribbon on each side of the elastic.

Step #2: Knot your two ends of ribbon around the elastic.

Step #3: Fold each end of the ribbon into a loop to create bow loops.

Step #4: Cross the left loop over the right loop. Then take the left loop under the right loop and pull tight. (Basically—tie a bow!)

Step 5: Arrange the ribbon loops. Each loop should be the same size. Cut the ends so they are the same length. (You can use clear nail polish to seal the ends.)

Step 6: Wrap the elastic around your ponytail and get ready to show your bow off to the world!

Bonus Step! JoJo's signature bow is actually a *double* bow. To make your bow into a double bow, use an extra long piece of ribbon. When you tie your first bow, leave enough ribbon on the ends for a second bow. Repeat steps three, four, and five to double your bow!

Rock a bow with as much flair as JoJo!

JOJO FACT

- Before JoJo appeared on *Abby's Ultimate Dance Competition* (AUDC), her mom had forty custom bows made to match the forty custom outfits she needed for the show!

14

MAKE A BOW TIE—FOR YOUR DAD, BROTHER, DOG—OR YOURSELF!

JoJo loves her hair bows—but they're not for everyone!
Maybe you're just not a ribbon type of girl (or guy!).
We think a bow tie is an excellent alternative to a
hair bow. Try making your own!

A bow tie makes
an excellent gift—for
your dad, your brother,
even your pup!

Let's tie this up!

Step #1: Find some fabric.

You can buy some at the fabric store or use some scraps from an old art project. (Luckily, bow ties don't require a lot of fabric.) Maybe you have an old shirt lying around that you can cut up for your bow tie. (Just make sure you have a parent's permission before you start cutting!)

Step #2: Cut the fabric into two pieces.

The first piece should be about a 5 x 7–inch rectangle—though you can make your tie bigger or smaller by making the rectangle bigger or smaller.

The second piece should be a square and smaller than the first piece. You'll use this to make the ring around the middle of the bow tie. You can use the same type of fabric or something different if you want to mix things up!

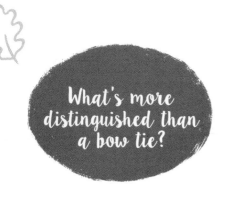

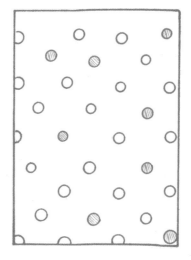

What's more distinguished than a bow tie?

Step #3: Start folding.

Fold the rectangle into thirds lengthwise. Rub some glue along the seam to get it to stay in place.

Fold the smaller piece of fabric into thirds and glue it together too.

Find the center of the larger piece and fold the ends so that they meet in the middle. Glue them into place. Then pinch the middle of the fabric together. See how it's starting to look like a bow tie?

let's tie this up!

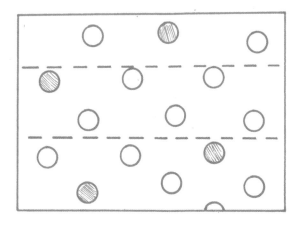

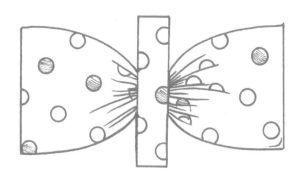

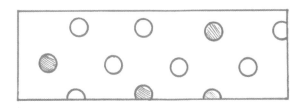

That's a wrap!

Step #4: That's a wrap!

Wrap the small piece of fabric around the pinch in the middle of the tie and then secure it with glue on the back of the bow.

Step #5: Clip it on.

Attach a clip to the back of the bow tie to make it into a clip-on tie. Clip it to your brother's shirt, your dog's collar, or wherever else strikes your fancy!

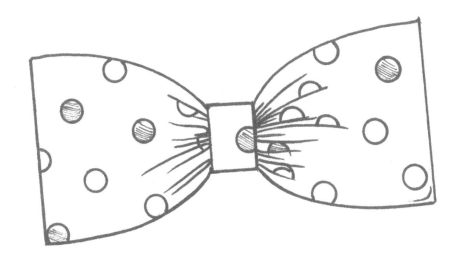

15

Reach Out to a Classmate Who's Being Bullied

Siwanatorz stand up to bullies. Some people stand up to bullies by bullying them back, but that's *not* what Siwanatorz do. Instead, we go up to the bully and politely say, "You shouldn't be doing this. It's wrong."

Unfortunately, that's not always enough to get a bully to stop bullying. This is when it's really important to tell a grown-up what's going on. Find an adult you trust—a teacher, a parent, or a counselor—and tell them what's going on. An adult will know how to help the person who is being bullied.

Reach out!

Even after you've stood up to the bully—even after you've talked to a grown-up—your work isn't finished! A true Siwanator will also reach out to the person who's been bullied. Here are a few things you can do to make someone feel better.

Option #1: Invite them over after school. It might seem like a small thing, but it will make their day!

Option #2: Sit with them at lunchtime. The school cafeteria can be a lonely place for a kid who's being bullied.

Option #3: Stand beside them. Pretend the bully isn't even there, and ask them about your teacher's latest assignment, their outfit, or the weather. You might feel a little weird at first, but by starting a new conversation, you're creating a distraction from the bullying. It really helps!

Helping someone else is always the right thing to do.

Option #4: Make them a gift! Print out a selfie of the two of you together to remind your friend that she's not alone.

Hi!

MESSAGE FROM JOJO

"Hey, what's wrong?
Come hang out with me!"

It can be scary
to speak up, but
Siwanatorz are
brave!

Winter
(December–February)

1

Winter Word Scramble

Winter is here! It's time for holiday cheer, snow days, and snowball fights. Let's celebrate the season by unscrambling a few of our favorite winter words!

Can you unscramble these winter words?

DOLC ______________________

ZZBDLIAR ______________________

WNOS YDA ______________________

ICCLIE ______________________

STFOR ______________________

TINVEAENL ______________________

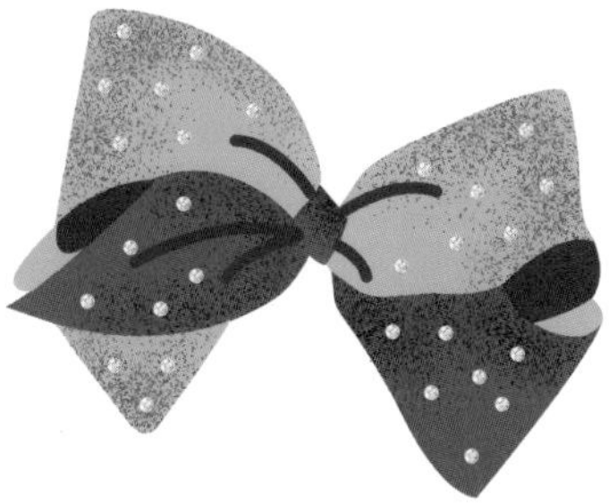

Answers: cold, blizzard, snow day, icicle, frost, Valentine

2

DECORATE YOUR HOUSE TO CELEBRATE THE SEASON

JoJo and her family are really close, and they do all sorts of activities together, including celebrating the holidays! One of their favorite traditions is picking a different theme for their Christmas tree each year. Start your own holiday tradition with themed decorations!

<del>JOJO</del> JAYDEN FACTS

....

- One year the Siwas chose sneakers because JoJo's brother, Jayden, loves sneakers so much!

- Jayden is a sneakerhead!

Anything goes when it comes to picking a theme, as long as it's something personal and unique to you and your family. But just in case you need a little inspiration, here are a few ideas to get you started!

Idea #1: Winter
Bring the snow inside! Use cotton to create the illusion of a snowbank on your mantel. Use glitter and tinsel to make it look like there are icicles dripping down the railing on your stairs. (Just make sure you have your parents' permission first—this can get messy!) Use twinkle lights to imitate the look of moonlight reflecting on your shiny icicles. Winter is here, so highlight the season!

Idea #2: Spring
Okay, we know we just said winter, but cold weather isn't necessarily everyone's cup of tea. So if you're one of those people, you can decorate your house to simulate springtime! Make plants and flowers out of construction paper and hang them up everywhere. Better yet, gather a bunch of potted plants to create an indoor garden.

Show the world you're a Siwanator!

Idea #3: Bows!

Bows are the best decoration—on people *or* trees! Make a dozen of them (see page 39 for instructions on how) and hang them like ornaments on your Christmas tree. Don't have a Christmas tree? Hang them from coat hooks, doorknobs, or anywhere else that strikes your fancy.

Anything goes when it comes to finding the right theme!

Idea #4: Your Favorite Thing

Do you have a favorite book? A favorite activity (like JoJo and dance)? A favorite TV show? Celebrate it! Print out excerpts from your favorite book in funky fonts and hang them up like pictures around the house. Take your tap shoes and turn them into an ornament. Cut out pictures of your favorite TV stars from magazines and create a one-of-a-kind collage. This is your chance to celebrate not just the season but also your favorite things, so go crazy! Even better—surprise your sibling with decorations devoted to his or her favorite thing!

MESSAGE FROM JOJO

"Nothing is ever 'typical' at our house!"

3

Peace!

Joy!

"PICTURE" YOUR HOLIDAY PRESENTS

The holiday season is about peace, joy, and spending time with our families. But we look forward to the gifts too! Did you know that giving presents is every bit as much fun as getting presents? And if you want the presents you give to be even more special, make them personal. What's more personal than a framed photograph?

Presents!

Step #1: Take the photograph.

Maybe you already have one photo that you love. Maybe you want to frame a photo from when you were really little or from the first day of school. That's great! But if you're interested in framing a new picture, we say, take a selfie! Is the present for your parents? Take a selfie with them or with your brother or sister, or with the whole family all together! Is the gift for your friends? Take a fun selfie with them. Make goofy faces or strike a pose—whatever captures your friendship best!

Step #2: Print the picture.

If you don't have a printer that can print photographs, that's okay. Maybe your school has one or one of your friends does. If not, there are websites that let you upload your photos and then send you a glossy print. (Just make sure you have your parents' permission first!)

Step #3: Pick out the perfect frame.

You can go to the store and buy a frame, or you can make one yourself. There are lots of different ways to do this: You can redecorate an old frame or make one out of Popsicle sticks (our personal favorite). You can even make a picture frame by cutting a picture-size opening in the cover of an old hardcover book. (Just make sure no one wants it anymore!)

Step #4: Give, give, give!

The great thing about this kind of gift is that you can make one (or a bunch!) for everyone and give new pictures over and over again. Sharing special photos is the kind of gift that never gets boring and always makes the recipient feel special.

Bonus idea: Instead of framing them, hang your pictures by using a piece of string and some clothespins: Tie the string across the room and use the clothespins to hang a bunch of different pictures across it.

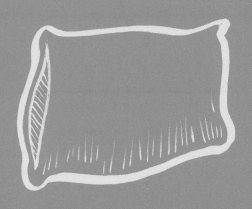

4

WISH THE NEW YEAR A HAPPY BIRTHDAY WITH A SLUMBER PARTY!

We think New Year's Eve is the perfect time to throw a slumber party for your best friends. But this isn't just any slumber party—it's a birthday party! Wish the New Year a happy birthday with your friends. Here are a few tips from JoJo.

Happy
New Year!

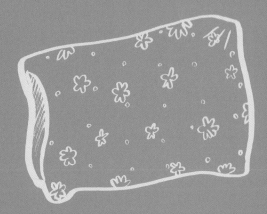

Party-Planning Tips!

Tip #1: Invite your friends.

You can print paper invitations and distribute them at school before winter break or put them in the mail. You can email your friends or design an online invitation. And don't just invite your best friends. You could also extend an invitation to a classmate who's a bit of an introvert, so she will feel included too. Or, if your friends are out of town for the holiday, celebrate the new year with your family instead!

Tip #2: Make the perfect playlist.

Every party needs the perfect playlist to get all your guests to dance and sing with you! Pick your favorite songs, such as the newest song they won't stop playing on the radio or an old song that your parents love to sing. Keep the tunes upbeat and fun. This is a birthday party, after all!

Tip #3: Bake a cake.

You can't exactly decorate a cake with two thousand and nineteen or twenty candles (depending on what year it is). You would need the world's biggest cake to fit that many! Instead, try three candles: one to mark the end of the passing year, one to mark the new year, and one for all the years yet to come.

Tip #4: Stay up till midnight.

Make sure your parents say it's okay to stay up, but what's a New Year's Eve party without the countdown as midnight approaches? Watch the clock, and count down to the New Year with the rest of the world—10, 9, 8, 7, 6, 5, 4, 3, 2, 1. But instead of shouting "Happy New Year" when you hit zero, shout "Happy Birthday," of course!

Tip #5: Sing "Happy Birthday."

At most New Year's Eve parties, after the clock strikes midnight, people sing an old song called "Auld Lang Syne." It's a beautiful song based on a poem written in 1788, and, no offense to the people who like to sing it, but this year, you're ringing in the New Year with a different soundtrack. Wish the New Year a happy birthday by singing "Happy Birthday" with your friends.

Party time!

Happy birthday New Year!

5

New Year's Resolutions!

New Year's resolutions are goals people set for the coming year. You can pick pretty much anything. New Year's resolutions are personal—they're *yours*. But here are a few resolutions we can all agree to strive for every year and every day.

Learn something new!

Resolve to be the best person you can be!

Resolution #1: Spend quality time with your parents.

JoJo doesn't live with her dad and brother full-time, so when they do get together, JoJo and her dad like to spend quality time together. It doesn't have to be anything fancy—JoJo and her dad love to play Dr. Mario on their old Nintendo system! It's really about setting aside uninterrupted time to be together.

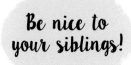

Resolution #2: Be nice to your siblings.

Let's face it—whether you have an older brother or a younger sister or both or some other combination of siblings—brothers and sisters can get on one another's nerves from time to time. But we love our siblings, and it's important not to forget to be nice to one another.

Resolution #3: Stand up to bullies.

This is something that every Siwanator takes seriously! If there's a bully in your class at school, resolve to stand up to them. Politely say that what he or she is doing wrong. And if that doesn't work, talk to a grown-up—a parent, teacher, or counselor—who can help.

Resolution #4: Try something new.

JoJo always wanted to dance, but she wanted to do a lot of other stuff too! So when she was six, she decided to try playing softball, and it turned out, she loved it! She's still trying out new sports all the time, like basketball and football. She likes to challenge herself. Eventually, she had to give up the softball team to make more time for dance, but she made amazing friends and learned a new skill. Trying something new is almost always rewarding.

What are *your* resolutions for the New Year?

Work
hard at
school!

_____

_____

_____

_____

_____

_____

_____

_____

_____

_____

_____

_____

_____

_____

Quality
time!

_____

_____

_____

Snow day!

Snowball fights!

6

Make Real Snow Cones!

This year, spend part of your snow day making real snow cones using actual snow! Live somewhere warm like Los Angeles, where JoJo lives? Use chopped or shaved ice instead!

Snowmen!

Hot chocolate!

Snow Cone Recipe!

Ingredients:
- An ice cream scoop
- Food coloring
- Juice or syrup—pick your favorite flavor!

Step #1: Head out into the snow with your ice cream scoop. Make sure you pick new, undisturbed snow. You're going to be eating this, so you want it to be as fresh and clean as possible.

Step #2: Use the scoop to spoon snow into a cup or glass.

Step #3: Pour on the flavor! Use your favorite kind of juice or syrup, or mix a couple of flavors together to get it just right. But don't take your time—the snow will melt quickly!

Step #4: Bon appétit!

Brr!

Yum!

7

Plant a Paper Garden While You Wait for Spring

Winter can be magical, but sometimes it feels like spring is never going to come. Remind yourself that spring is just around the corner by "planting" a paper garden in your bedroom. Start with these tissue-paper roses!

Spring is just around the corner!

Make Tissue-Paper Roses

Step #1: Start with tissue paper. Use whatever color you want your roses to be.

Step #2: Cut the paper into squares, about six inches by six inches (or bigger, if you want bigger flowers!). Stack eight squares on top of each other. You can even make multicolored roses by layering different colors!

Step #3: Fold the paper accordion style.

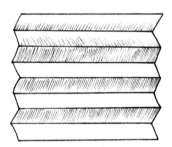

Step #4: Twist a green pipe cleaner around the center of your accordion. This will hold the center of your rose together and act as a stem! (Luckily, these roses won't have thorns!)

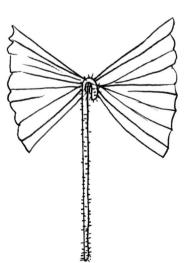

Step #5: Carefully start to separate the layers of the rose on one side of the pipe cleaner. Fluff them until they look like half a flower. Then do the same thing to the layers on the other side.

Step #6: Fill a pot or a vase with your paper roses and look forward to spring!

Bonus Step: If you want to make your rose even fancier, add one more step between steps four and five: Trim the edges of your accordion folds so that they look more like petals—you can go with a round edge, a little bit pointy, even a couple of curves, or shred the edges for a rougher look.

Extra Bonus Step: Spray the roses with perfume that smells like actual flowers to make them feel even more real! But spray lightly—you don't want the wet perfume weighing your "petals" down.

Everything's coming up roses!

Sprinkles!

8

Host a Cupcake Decorating Party for Valentine's Day!

Valentine's Day is all about celebrating love, and we don't just mean romantic love. It can be the love you feel for your family or friends. Celebrate with your friends by throwing a Valentine's Day party complete with the very best activity of all—decorating cupcakes!

Frosting!

Here are a few tips for hosting the greatest cupcake decorating party EVER!

Tip #1: Obviously, you need cupcakes. You can make them from a mix or bake them from scratch if you're feeling particularly ambitious. If you're baking them yourself, be sure to use fun cupcake liners—choose pink, red, and white if you can. After all, it is Valentine's Day!

Tip #2: Frosting is key. Buy delicious flavors in cool colors. Make sure you have enough for everyone. Put each different color into a bowl along with a spoon so that your guests can help themselves. (Also, frosting is sticky, so it will help the rest of your decorations stay in place.)

Delicious!

Tip #3: Don't stop at frosting! Add sprinkles. Lots of sprinkles. Try to find red, white, and pink for the holiday, or even heart-shaped sprinkles. Line the containers of sprinkles up on the kitchen counter or dining room table (wherever your parents say it's okay) so your friends can pick and choose their favorites.

Tip #4: What else do you want on your cupcake? How about mini marshmallows? Or chocolate chips? Or mini peanut butter cups? Get a variety so that you and your friends will have lots to choose from.

Spread the love!

Tip #5: This is Valentine's Day, so spread the love! If you decorate more cupcakes than you can eat, your friends can bring their extras home to share with their families. Or you can bring some cupcakes to school to share with your classmates! Just make sure there's enough for everyone so no one feels left out.

Love and Cupcakes!

MESSAGE FROM JOJO

"If you want really good friends, you've got to be a really good friend!"

Be Mine

9

Valentine's Day Word Game!

There's nothing more fun than making your friends and family laugh. Telling a good joke can even make *you* laugh, even though you know the punch line all along. So in honor of Valentine's Day, here's a word game to make your friends—and yourself—laugh.

Without telling your friends anything about the story below, ask them to help you fill in the blanks with the words indicated below each blank—a name, a noun, a verb, etc. Chances are, when you read back the story with the blanks filled in, it will be hilarious!

Valentine's Day is the best. It gives everyone an excuse to eat _____
name of food

and exchange _____.
type of gift

_____was pretty excited for Valentine's Day. In fact, she'd already
girl's name
picked out the cards she was going to give to her best friends. They had a

picture of a _____ on them. She knew her friends would love them!
noun

She was also going to surprise her friends with _____. What could
type of food
be more delicious?

But she began to worry that if she only gave cards and treats to her friends,

the rest of the kids in her class would feel left out. So she decided to bake

enough _____ to share with her whole class. She was up all night
same type of food
baking, but it was worth it. She even made extra for her teacher and her

family—delicious!

She decorated her _____ with _____, _____ ,
same type of food   noun   noun

and _____. They looked amazing! She
                  noun
couldn't wait to share them with everyone.

On Valentine's Day morning, she surprised the

whole class with her cards and _____.
                                      same type of food
Her teacher, Mrs. _____, let the whole
                        last name
class take a break to gobble up their goodies.

A few days later, the whole class surprised her

with a treat of their own—a freshly baked

_____. It was delicious too!
new type of food

_____ knew that this was the real magic
same girl's name
of Valentine's Day—spreading some love and

kindness and seeing it come back to you.

JOJO FACTS

· JoJo loves a good joke!

· From practical jokes to making prank calls, she and her friends have tried it all, and they're still laughing.

MESSAGE FROM JOJO

*"I love, love, love being funny.
It's my favorite thing!"*

Is the Winter Weather Getting You Down? Wear Something Special to Brighten Everyone's Day!

The end of winter can get long and dreary. One way to combat the winter doldrums is by wearing bright colors—and the fun doesn't have to stop there! JoJo loves dressing up. Here are a few outfit ideas to brighten up the gray days of winter.

Bring some sunshine to wintertime!

Tips to Brighten Up the Gray Days of Winter!

Tip #1: Switch out that woolen hat for a colorful bow.
We're not suggesting that you go bareheaded on a cold day, but maybe once you get to school you can duck into the bathroom and replace your hat with a colorful bow, just like JoJo would do. Trust us—the right bow can make any day feel special.

Tip #2: Wear a tutu.
Okay, we know this one sounds crazy, but when JoJo was little, she wore a tutu whether it was time to dance or not. Of course, it doesn't have to be a tutu—do you love soccer as much as JoJo loves to dance? Then wear your favorite soccer jersey. Or maybe you love to ice skate—wear a skirt that spins out around you when you twirl on the ice. Find a way to bring your favorite activity into your everyday wardrobe.

Tip #3: Add some color!
Who says pastel pink is only for springtime? Or bright blue is only for summer? Or orange is just for the fall? Wear colorful clothes all year round—you will literally brighten up the landscape!

Tip #4: When all else fails, throw a costume party!
We already said that you don't need to wait for Halloween to dress up—and the middle of winter is the perfect time to remind yourself and your friends that there's always a reason to wear your favorite costume! Invite your friends over for a movie or a sleepover, but insist that everyone wear something special.

Still stuck for ideas? Choreograph a dance to a winter-themed song.

Lighten up!

Glide across the ice!

11

Learn to Ice Skate or Teach a Friend

JoJo loves learning, and she's not intimidated by skills that take a long time to master. She believes that learning something new is a lot of fun, even when it's a lot of work.

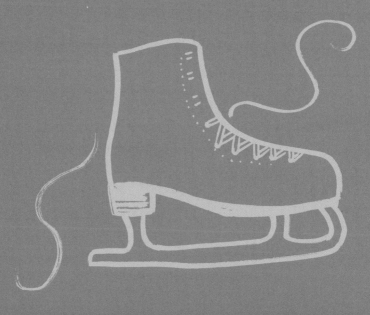

Ice skating can be tricky. You have to be balanced and brave to stay upright. Here are a few tips that will help you learn. In fact, these tips are great advice for learning anything new.

Tip #1: Take a correction and apply it.
If someone's correcting you, it's not an insult. It's that person's way of trying to help! It means she's paying attention and wants you to get better. Your teacher can see things differently than you can, so take the correction and apply it to your next step. Trust your teacher. There's a reason she's the one teaching you!

Tip #2: Don't be embarrassed.
Whether it's ice skating, dancing, or singing, it's hard not to be scared that we might mess up and look foolish when trying something new. While learning to ice skate, you might literally fall down in front of everyone! But nobody is perfect at anything the first time they try it.

Twirl! Jump! Spin!

Tip #3: Practice.

If you want to learn a new skill, you have to practice. But trust us—if it's something you want to learn, practicing won't feel like work! Getting better over time is part of the fun.

Tip #4: Be brave.

Learning new things can seem scary at first. Most of the time, you have to work really hard to become good at something you've never tried before. But here's the secret: You *will* become good at it. The first time you strap on a pair of skates, it may feel impossible just to stand up! But if you work hard and listen to your teacher, eventually you'll be gliding across the ice.

JOJO FACTS

• It took JoJo a whole year to learn how to edit music on her computer, but at the end of that year, she'd produced her own song!

• The first song JoJo produced by herself was the JoJo's Juice song.

• JoJo is now something of a technology expert, editing YouTube videos and creating thumbnails.

MESSAGE FROM JOJO

"Find whatever interests you and go after it. Learn as much as you can about it!"

12

Create a Friendship-Trivia Game

Invite your squad over for an evening of games. Just don't tell them that tonight's game is going to be all about *them*. That's right. You're creating your very own friendship-trivia game! Not only is it a ton of fun, but it can be a great way for your different friends to get to know each other.

How well do your friends know you?

Here are a few ideas for questions in your friendship-trivia game! You might discover that there's more than one correct answer to a question. Maybe two or three of your friends are big readers or dancers or singers. Chances are you guys have a lot in common. After all, that's part of why you became friends in the first place!

Idea #1: Who's most likely to be found curled up with a good book?

Idea #2: Who's most likely to be found making a video of her latest dance moves?

Idea #3: Who's the class clown?

Idea #4: Who has the most brothers and sisters?

Idea #5: Who's an only child?

Idea #6: Who's most likely to be an expert at the latest technology?

Idea #7: Who has the most followers on social media?

Idea #8: Who loves to sing?

Idea #9: Who's the biggest JoJo fan?

But don't stop there—create your own list of questions that are specific to your friends.

_____

_____

_____

_____

_____

MESSAGE FROM JOJO

"I have a lot of new friends in addition to the old ones who went through changes with me."

13

Throw a Family Game Night!

One great way to spend time with your family is to throw a family game night. Put down your devices, turn off the TV, and just spend some good, old-fashioned quality time together.

Family Game Night!

JOJO FACTS

- When the four Siwas are together, they try to make it special!

- The girls (that's JoJo and her mom) live in California while the boys (JoJo's brother, Jayden, and her dad) live in Nebraska.

Here are a few tips to make sure your family game night is a hit.

Tip #1: Snacks!
What's a game night without snacks? Make some popcorn and put out some chips and dip and a little bit of candy. You can even set the candy aside as a prize for the winners!

Tip #2: Games!
Every family game night needs games. What are your family's favorites? Do you like to quiz each other with trivia? Prefer to race your way around a board game? Or combine the two to create a game that's all your own! For example, you can invent a rule that a player can't roll the dice on a board game until they correctly answer a trivia question.

Tip #3: Teams!
Even the closest of families can get a little competitive, and one way to take the competition to the next level is to play in teams. Maybe you and your sibling team up against your parents, or you and your dad can team up against your mom and your sibling. Pick whatever combination sounds best to you! And next time you throw a family game night, you can choose different teams to mix it up!

Tip #4: Have fun!
No matter how much you want to win, remember that the point of a family game night is to spend time together. So don't take the competition too seriously. We know it sounds corny, but everyone in the family will feel like a winner if you all have a good time together.

MESSAGE FROM JOJO

"Our family is always laughing. We love to tease each other!"

87

14

CREATE A MANTRA

Life has taught JoJo that if you want to do well and be successful, you have to <u>believe in yourself</u>. The best way to succeed is to start a task thinking, "I'm going to be amazing." It will make you feel better and make any activity more fun!

Be confident!

One way to help keep your confidence high is to create a mantra, a saying you repeat to yourself when you need a boost. Here are a few ideas to help you get started.

I am powerful!
I am smart!
I am brave!
I am a Siwanator!

But the best mantras are personal—they're about what *you* want to be. So try creating your own mantra.

I am _____

I am _____

I am _____

I am _____

I am _____

I am _____

I am _____

I am _____

And, if you're still feeling low, close your eyes and remind yourself of all the things you want to be.

Be happy!
Be creative!
Be kind!
Be silly!

What else do you want to be?

Be . . . _____

Be . . . _____

Be . . . _____

Be . . . _____

Be . . . _____

Be . . . _____

Be . . . _____

Be . . . _____

Believe in yourself!

MESSAGES FROM JOJO

"When people ask me what my best advice is, I say, 'Believe in yourself!'"

"Whenever I'm feeling down, I tell myself, 'my name is JOJO Siwa. I've got this.'"

"Siwanatorz are strong, confident, and powerful!"

15

Interview an Older Relative

Sometimes it can be hard to actually *relate* to some of the people we're related to! When your grandmother was your age, she probably didn't have email, let alone smartphones and YouTube videos! But you might have more in common with some of the older members of your family than you realize. You just have to ask!

The one who asks the most questions learns the most!

Next time you see your grandmother, aunt, uncle, dad, or grandfather, ask him or her to sit down for an interview. Act like a real reporter: Come prepared with a list of questions, and take notes on their answers. Before you know it, you might discover that you have more in common than you ever imagined!

Not sure how to get started? Don't worry. We've got you covered! Here are some questions to help get your interview going.

Where did you live when you were my age?

Did you have a computer when you were my age?

What did you and your friends do together when you were my age?

What was your favorite food when you were my age?

When did you have your first date? Your first kiss?

What was your favorite outfit when you were my age?

Did you and your parents get along when you were my age?

Did you and your siblings get along when you were my age?

Were you close to your grandmother when you were my age?

What did you want to be when you grew up?

What do you have in
common with your grandmother?
. . . with your dad?
. . . with your great-aunt?
. . . with your uncle?
. . . with your grandfather?

Just ask!

Spring

(March–May)

1

Springtime Word Scramble

Spring is here! It's time for budding flowers, leaves on trees, spring cleaning, and the end of school. Let's get in the mood for springtime with a few of our favorite spring words.

Can you unscramble these spring words?

FFODADLIS _____

GNIEACLN _____

UOTPSRS _____

RADGEN _____

NIGRPS RWFOADR _____

CLOOSH SNDE _____

2

Plant a Garden (Inside or out!)

Spring is the perfect time to start a garden. So start digging!

Tips for Planting Your Spring Garden

Tip #1: Pick your place and your plants.
Are you claiming a patch of the backyard for your garden? Reserving a spot in your neighborhood community garden? Are you gathering pots for an indoor herb garden in your kitchen? Wherever you're planting, make sure there's enough sunshine (or shade) for the kind of plants you want to grow.

That brings us to picking your plants! Spring is a great time to plant herbs like basil, mint, lavender, and thyme. Strawberries and blueberries are delicious backyard treats. Tomatoes get planted in springtime, but they won't be ready for eating until later in summer, so be patient!

Tip #2: Gather your supplies.
Ask your parents to help you gather fertilizer, garden soil, and tools like a shovel, a trowel, and work gloves.

Tip #3: Prepare your seeds.
If you're planting seeds (instead of plants), germinate them in a wet paper towel until they sprout. Then put the sprouted seeds and some potting soil into a small container and keep it in a sunny area inside your house until you see seedlings. Don't have gardening pots? You can improvise with empty yogurt cups with a hole punched in the bottom!

Tip #4: Prepare the soil.
If you're planting in your yard or a community garden, you're going to need to prepare the soil—clearing rocks and pulling weeds that might be there. Make sure you dig out the weeds completely! When your soil is soft and free of debris, you can add garden soil or fertilizer, if you're using either.

Grow potted plants indoors!

Tip #5: Start planting!

Dig a hole in your prepared soil, then put the plant or seed in. Cover it with soil, water as needed, and be sure to keep an eye out for weeds. Watch your sprouts turn into plants!

Fun Twists on Spring Cleaning

Spring is the perfect time of year for a fresh start, and
what could be fresher than a clean slate?

Embrace a
clean slate!
Give yourself a
fresh start!

Prepare yourself to thrive!

Here are some fun ways to get a fresh start this spring.

Idea #1: Redecorate your room.
We're not talking about getting a new bedspread and fresh carpet. (That kind of thing is usually up to our parents, anyway!) But there are smaller things you can do to make your room feel brand-new. Maybe you have a lot of pictures and posters on your walls. Switching them out with new pictures and posters—or even just moving around the ones you have—can make a big difference. One of our favorite ways to redecorate is by rearranging our bookshelves. You can arrange your books by color, by theme, or by author. Maybe you want to leave more room to display framed pictures and your favorite knickknacks. Whatever you choose, we promise that rearranging your room will make a big impact!

Idea #2: Revamp your wardrobe.
Instead of thinking of it as cleaning out your closet, think of it as a chance to revamp your wardrobe! Try on clothes that you haven't worn in a while. Do they still fit? Does this dress or that pair of pants still feel like *you*? If the answer is no, then let those old clothes go! And, as a bonus, you'll be creating more space in your closet and drawers to accumulate new clothes that do feel right. But leave space for an outfit or two that might not fit anymore but that might have sentimental value, like an old Halloween costume that can still give you a fright or the dress you wore for a special occasion when you were little.

Idea #3: Refresh your accessories.
How many ribbons and bows has JoJo accumulated over the years? We may never know! Hang on to a few items that are meaningful to you, but if there's something you don't want to wear anymore, now is the perfect time to let it go. Best of all, going through bedside drawers and jewelry boxes, you might come across an accessory—a pair of earrings, a super cool hair bow—that you used to love and have forgotten about. Maybe you'll find something old that you want to start wearing again. Sometimes, that's even better than buying something new!

Bonus Idea: Give someone else a fresh start.
Maybe when you rearranged your bookshelves, you set aside a few books you don't want anymore. Or maybe while you were cleaning out your closet, you came across some clothes that you've outgrown. Spring cleaning isn't just an opportunity to give yourself a clean slate. It's also a chance to be generous. Find a local charity that accepts donations of clothing and books to bring your fresh start to the next level!

Don't think of it as cleaning—think of it as redecorating, revamping, and refreshing!

4

Celebrate Siblings Day

Siblings Day falls every April 10, and it's an excellent opportunity to carve out a little sibling-on-sibling quality time. Or, if you're an only child, spend time with someone who's like a brother or sister to you, like a cousin or good friend.

A few ideas for spending time with your siblings!

Idea #1: Throw a party with both of your friends—and mix everyone together.
When JoJo still lived in Omaha, her brother would throw parties for his baseball friends, and JoJo would invite her dance friends to join, and everyone would end up all mixed together! Not only did JoJo and Jayden get to throw a party together, but their friends got to meet each other and become friends too.

Idea #2: Solve a puzzle together.
JoJo and Jayden love going to escape rooms, which are really popular in Los Angeles. You get locked in a room for an hour and have to uncover all the clues to unlock the door before time runs out! The clues are super hard, but sometimes solving a puzzle together is a great way to bond with someone. And, of course, it doesn't have to be an escape room! It can be finishing a crossword puzzle together or putting together a jigsaw puzzle. What matters is that you're solving a problem together.

Idea #3: Try each other's favorite things.
Jayden loves playing baseball every bit as much as JoJo loves to dance. A good way to get closer to someone is to try out the thing he or she loves most. It's great for siblings to have their own interests, but a nice way to show someone how much they mean to you is to be interested in the things they're interested in!

Idea #4: Teach each other something.
There's another great thing about siblings trying out each other's favorite things—it gives them a chance to show each other how to do something. Maybe you love to dance (like JoJo!), and your big brother has two left feet. That doesn't mean you can't have a great time trying to teach him your latest moves! Don't take it too seriously, though. You're just teaching each other for fun, so remember to laugh!

JOJO FACTS

Idea #5: Cheer each other on.
When JoJo is in Omaha, one of her favorite things to do is watch her brother play baseball. In fact, she and her mom plan their trips to Omaha around Jayden's games so they can be in the stands to cheer him on. We should all try to be our siblings' biggest fans, just like JoJo is for Jayden.

- Did you know JoJo and Jayden's birthdays are only one day apart?

- JoJo loves spending time with her brother so much that she went to school with Jayden for a day just to get to be with him!

MESSAGE FROM JOJO

"Sometimes Jayden and I get mad at each other, but we really don't fight. We just know it's wrong, so we don't do it—easy as that!"

5

HOST A MOTHER/DAUGHTER TEA PARTY FOR MOTHER'S DAY

Moms do so much for us, and that's one reason why it's great that Mother's Day comes around every May—a whole day to celebrate our moms! Don't stop at your mom—maybe your best friend's mom always has your favorite dessert when you come over for dinner, or your aunt or your grandma is like a mom to you too. Celebrate all the moms in your life by hosting a very special Mother/Daughter Tea Party on Mother's Day!

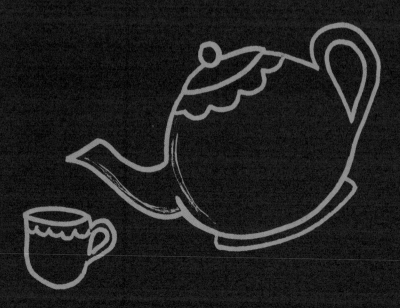

Tips for Hosting the Greatest Mother/Daughter Tea Party Ever!

Tip #1: Send out printed invitations.
We know it's old-fashioned, but there's nothing quite like getting a printed invitation in the mail. Ask everyone to RSVP so that you know how much tea and snacks you'll need!

Tip #2: Dress up.
If you ask us, teatime is an excellent excuse to wear pretty pastel colors and lots of ruffles and bows. (You know how JoJo feels about bows!)

Tip #3: Snack appropriately.
The traditional snacks for a tea party are things like scones with clotted cream and cucumber sandwiches. You don't have to be quite that traditional, but you can still make the food you serve special. If you're offering your guests sandwiches, cut them into finger sandwich–size pieces to make them seem fancier.

Tip #4: Enlist some help from your dad.
One potential problem with hosting an event on Mother's Day is that it might end up meaning more work for your mom, which is the last thing you want! So ask your dad or another grown-up to help with setting up and cleaning up.

Tip #5: A teatime toast.
Wait until all of your guests arrive. Then ask everyone to lift their teacups in honor of all the moms, aunts, sisters, and friends who are there. Thank these wonderful women for all they do to support you every day!

JOJO FACTS

* JoJo and her mom are really close. They're basically best friends!

* Jessalynn never forced JoJo to dance or sing. But when JoJo decided what she wanted, her mom was always there to support JoJo's goals!

MESSAGE FROM JOJO

"My mom was that person who always knew what I needed, when I needed it, and how to help."

6

Customize Your Favorite T-Shirt!

Most of us don't have TV appearances that require wearing custom-made outfits like JoJo does, but that doesn't mean we can't rock a one-of-a-kind style once in a while! Create your own utterly unique outfit by customizing your favorite T-shirt.

How to Make a One-Of-A-Kind T-Shirt

Step #1. Pick a T-shirt.
Make sure you have your parents' permission, especially if you're making changes to a shirt you already own and love. Another option is to buy a plain white T-shirt (or red, yellow, or pink—the color is up to you!) to work with. You can start with something totally boring, because once you're done, it's not going to be boring anymore!

Step #2. Gather supplies.
Puff paint? Check. Fabric markers? You got 'em. Glitter glue? Can't hurt. Fabric scissors? Check, check, check!

Step #3. Start customizing!
There are so many different ways to make a T-shirt one of a kind. Show the world you're a Siwanator by drawing an enormous bow across your T-shirt. Decorate the shirt with hashtags like #PeaceOutHaterz (JoJo's favorite) or #LuckyCharmedLife (another fave).

But don't stop with decorations. You can customize your T-shirt even more with a good pair of fabric scissors. Cut a curved pattern along the sleeves and hem to create ruffles. Turn a crewneck shirt into a V-neck. Turn a long-sleeved tee into a tank top!

Step #4. Make the world your runway.
Put your T-shirt on and strut your stuff! Remember, no one else in the world has a shirt like this one, so wear it with pride. Not only is your new shirt one of a kind, but you also designed it yourself—all the more reason to love it!

JOJO FACTS

- JoJo loves dressing up!

- When JoJo appeared on *AUDC*, her mom had the forty outfits custom made (with forty matching custom bows) for the show! And, because the outfits were custom-made, they were one of a kind just for JoJo.

MESSAGE FROM JOJO

"I've always loved dressing up!"

7

Rewrite the Rules on Game Day

Hosting a game day is a great way to bring friends and family together. You can play board games, parlor games (like charades and twenty questions), or, weather permitting, you can divide into teams and head to your backyard or the park to play dodgeball, red rover, and tag.

Still, sometimes the same old games can get a little bit boring. So take your game night to the next level by switching up the rules for the games you already know and love.

Remember—winning isn't everything!

Tips for Your Next Game Day

Tip #1: Combine hide-and-seek with tag.
This time, whoever's "it" doesn't just have to find where everyone else is hiding. He or she has to catch them too!

Tip #2: Combine trivia and dodgeball.
You know the basic rules to dodgeball: two teams, a bunch of balls, and trying to avoid getting hit by balls thrown by the opposite team. But what if you have a chance to save yourself even after you've been hit by a ball? Ask a friend or grown-up to sit on the sidelines and ask players trivia questions when they are hit by the ball. If the players answer the questions correctly, they can stay in the game.

Tip #3: Mix up charades.
With a normal game of charades, you get a clue and have to act it out without using words. But what if you're *only* allowed to use words instead and you can't use any gestures at all! After you've read your clue, your teammates have to put on blindfolds, so they can't even see the expression on your face as you try to explain the clue.

Take game day to the next level!

Tip #4: Sing and dance.
You know how much JoJo loves to sing and dance, and chances are, if you're a Siwanator, singing and dancing are two of your favorite things too. So make singing and dancing part of your next game night! Start by playing one of your favorite board games, but every time someone rolls the dice, you put on one of your favorite songs for a few seconds and then turn it off. Whoever rolled the dice has to sing the rest of the verse (and even dance along) before moving his or her piece across the board. Don't know the words? Then you lose a turn. Just make sure you're playing songs that your friends are likely to know the lyrics to. Otherwise it's not fair!

Do you have some ideas to improve your favorite game-day activities? List them here!

_____

_____

_____

_____

_____

_____

_____

_____

_____

_____

_____

_____

_____

MESSAGE FROM JOJO

"'Family' can be defined a million different ways!"

How about a makeover with your best friend?

8

MAKEOVERS!

There are lots of different ways to give yourself a makeover. Brand-new clothes? Check. Brand-new make-up? Check. Brand-new attitude? Check!

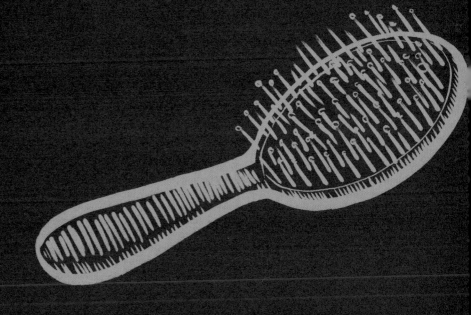

· ·

- When JoJo has a big performance, having a special outfit, makeup, and hairdo helps her feel ready to go onstage and give it her all.

When you love what you're wearing, it can make you feel more confident, inside and out!

Give yourself a makeover!

Idea #1: Try a new hairstyle.

Maybe you've had the same haircut for as long as you can remember and you're finally ready to mix it up. Or maybe there's an elaborate updo you've always wanted to try. Well, now's your chance! Make appointments for you and your mom, your BFF, big sister, or someone else close to you at your local hair salon, and get ready to try something new. Bring pictures from magazines of your favorite celebrities, so you can show the stylist what you have in mind. Or, if you're feeling particularly brave, tell the stylist that you're in her hands and she can do whatever she thinks looks best!

Idea #2: Experiment with makeup.

Most of us don't get to have our makeup done by professionals like JoJo does before a big performance or TV appearance. But that doesn't mean we can't get tips from the pros! A great way to learn about makeup is to ask someone at one of the makeup counters in your local mall to give you some lessons. It's a lot of fun, and it's usually free. (Just make sure you're up-front with the makeup artist if you're not planning to buy anything!)

Idea #3: Host a fashion show.

Maybe there are some old clothes in the back of your closet that you haven't worn for years because they're just not your style anymore. Maybe you've been hanging on to a favorite sweatshirt that you've long since outgrown.

Invite your friends over for a fashion show and try on the outfits that you can't decide whether or not to keep. Put on some music and strut across your bedroom like it's your own private runway! Let your friends vote on what you should keep and what needs to go. You can donate your old clothes to charity!

Idea #4: Try something new.
We know, we know—we talk a lot about trying new things, but isn't that what makeovers are all about? Whether it's a new haircut, a new lip gloss, or a new outfit, it's really all about trying something new. But don't stop with the things that you can only see from the outside. Try learning something new—singing or dancing to a new song, making a new friend . . . The possibilities are endless!

MESSAGE FROM JOJO

"Once I had on my makeup and costume, I was ready!"

119

9

Host a Viewing Party for Your Favorite Show or Movie

Maybe there's a TV show that you and your friends can't get enough of, and the season finale is just around the corner. Or maybe your BFF *still* hasn't seen your favorite movie. Or maybe JoJo is about to release a new music video, and you and your friends cannot wait! Whatever the show, movie, or song, sometimes you want to share your favorite things with your friends.

Host the greatest viewing party EVER!

How to Host the Greatest Viewing Party Ever

Tip #1: Anybody can make popcorn, but can you create snacks that fit the theme of the show, movie, or song? Of course you can! If you're watching a romantic movie, serve heart-shaped cookies. Or maybe it's a horror film. Then serve cupcakes covered in white frosting, with chocolate chips for ghostly eyes.

Lights, Camera, Action!

Tip #2: Ask your guests to dress up to fit the theme of the show, movie, or song, and be sure to set an example with your own amazing costume. If you're watching a movie about vampires, get ready to bare your fangs. Or if it's a TV show set in a different time, dress in old-fashioned or futuristic clothing to match!

Tip #3: Quiz each other with trivia. If you're watching the season finale of your favorite show, create questions about what happened in the season so far. If it's the sequel to a beloved movie, ask questions about the first movie. Or maybe it's a movie adaptation of one of your favorite books. You can try to identify differences between the book and the movie.

Tip #4: But no talking during the show! When we get together with our friends, it can be hard to keep quiet. Maybe it's a movie everyone's seen before, and you can't watch it without quoting your favorite lines—that's okay! But if it's something new and you're worried you won't be able to hear the dialogue over the sound of your friends whispering, make sure you set some ground rules before you start the show. You can always press pause if there's something you've just got to say!

Snacks, Costumes, Trivia!

10

Start a Positive Trend on Social Media

JoJo loves social media. It's a great way for her to keep in touch with her fans and express herself. But like a lot of us, JoJo knows that, unfortunately, social media isn't all good. A long time ago, she decided to use her social media to make people feel *good* about themselves, and you can do the same! Maybe we can't stop the haters, but we *can* make social media a more positive place.

Siwanatorz believe in being positive—and that includes on their social media.

Start a positive trend! Tell someone you like their outfit, write an appreciative note to your best friend, or reach out to your favorite author to tell them how much you love their book.

Here are a few of JoJo's favorite—and very positive—hashtags to help you get started.

- #PeaceOutHaterz
- #SiwanatorzRule
- #FamilyMatters
- #WhenLifeThrowsACurveball
- #FriendsAreEverywhere
- #CalmCoolCollected
- #CantStopWontStop
- #LuckyCharmedLife

What really matters is how you feel about yourself—no matter what anyone says.

MESSAGE FROM JOJO

"If I could make people talk online . . . I could potentially make it positive."

"I'm different, but I've learned over time that being different is a good thing. I bet you're different in a good way too. And anyone who doesn't like it, well . . . I've got one thing to say: #PeaceOutHaterz!"

JOJO FACT

• When JoJo was on *AUDC*, she had her first brush with the downside of social media: Dozens of strangers said that they wanted JoJo eliminated in the next episode! They made fun of every part of her—not just her dancing, but also the way she looked and spoke.

125

Design your box with your mom, dad, sibling, or friends!

11

CREATE AN END-OF-SCHOOL MEMORY BOX

The school year may almost be over, but the memories you've made this year are sure to last a lifetime. Preserve them by creating an end-of-school memory box.

How to Make a Memory Box

You will need:

1. A box. (Of course!) You can buy a plain gift box from a crafts store, or repurpose an old shoebox.

2. Decorative paper, like wrapping paper or construction paper. (Get creative—you can use old newspaper or magazine articles too!)

3. Other decorations. It's your memory box, so pick decorations that fit the things you want to remember, whether it's a tough test you aced, a school performance you smashed, or a ribbon from a race you won.

4. Glue.

5. The mementoes you want to put inside: photographs, report cards, art projects, friendship bracelets. Pick the things that will bring back the most memories when you look through the box later.

Decorate and Save!

Step #1: Measure and cut the decorative paper so that it will cover each side of your box.

Step #2: Coat your box with glue, then attach the paper. Make sure you give the glue time to dry.

Step #3: Add decorations: photos, drawings, sequins, and stars. Be sure to label the box with your name and the dates or grade you're commemorating.

Step #4: Fill the box with your precious mementoes. Just think how much fun it will be to sift through all those memories in the years to come!

You don't have to keep your memories to yourself! Give your memory box as a gift—to your best friend, your teacher, your mom or dad, or your sibling!

12

End-of-School Thank-Yous

There are a lot of people who help us get through the school year: teachers, parents, siblings, and friends. As the school year comes to a close, it's the perfect time to take a few minutes to say thank you to all the people who helped make your year better.

Get started by making a gratitude list!

I am grateful to . . .

. . . my teachers.
Teachers can take many forms. Obviously, there's the person standing at the front of your classroom (unless you're homeschooled). But what about the gym teacher who helped you perfect your pitch? Or the dance teacher who's always en pointe? Maybe you met with a tutor to polish your math skills. Whoever your teachers are, they deserve a thank-you before the school year ends.

Which teachers will you thank this year?

_____

_____

_____

. . . my parents
Maybe your parents help you with your homework every night—even after they've had a full day of working hard! Maybe your mom bought all the supplies you needed for your art project or your dad came to every dance recital to cheer you on. Let your parents—or the people who are like parents to you—know how much you appreciate their support.

I'm grateful that my parents helped with . . .

_____

_____

_____

_____

. . . my siblings.

Maybe you have a big sister who helped you with the grammar lessons she mastered when she was your age. Or maybe your little sister is your biggest cheerleader, the way JoJo supports her brother, Jayden. Or maybe the cousin who's like a sibling to you is always there when you need her. Don't miss this chance to let your family know how grateful you are for their help!

I'm grateful that my sister/brother . . .

_____

_____

_____

. . . my friends.

Maybe you made a new friend this year, and you've become closer than you ever imagined. Or maybe your lifelong best friend was there for you every step of the way, just like always. Maybe you have friends outside of school that you didn't get to see as much as you would have liked, and you're excited to spend more time with them now that school is nearly over. Whatever the reason, let your friends know that you feel lucky to have them.

There are lots of ways to say thank you—on social media, in person, or even with a handwritten note.

Which friends will you thank?

_____

_____

_____

13

Make Friendship Bracelets for the Friends You Made This Year

The school year may be about the end, but here's hoping that the friendships you made this year will last a lifetime! A friendship bracelet is a great way to commemorate a new (or old) friendship.

Show your friends how much they mean to you!

Let's make friendship bracelets!

There are plenty of different ways to make bracelets. Try these fun and easy methods.

Method #1: Pick out some scrap fabric.
This can be fabric you buy at a crafts store or maybe something more personal, like an old shirt or a pair of PJ pants you wore to your last sleepover. Cut the fabric into long, thin rectangles. Then use a hole punch to create holes in the fabric. Then take a bracelet chain, ribbon, or piece of yarn and weave it through the holes to make a bracelet.

There's something so special about a gift that you make yourself!

Method #2: Make a delicious—if temporary!—bracelet using jelly beans, cereal, and candy.

Take some thread and loop it through a needle until it doubles over on itself. Then tie a knot at the end. Use the needle to string candy and treats along the thread. Cut the needle away, and then tie the ends of the thread together.

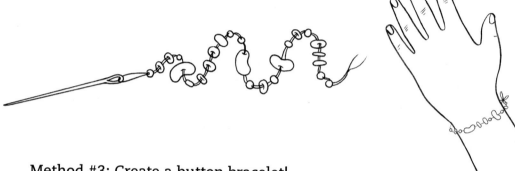

Method #3: Create a button bracelet!

Any buttons will do, but we suggest going to a crafts store to pick up buttons in each of your friends' favorite colors, along with matching string. You'll need buttons with four holes. Then, cut two pieces of string. Thread each end into one pair of buttonholes so that one piece of string is on each side. Before you pull the string tight through the holes, thread the ends of the string through the loop. This will help keep the button in place. Wrap the string around your wrist and tie the ends together!

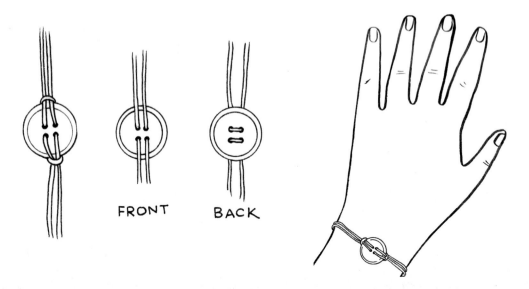

FRONT   BACK

14

Set Some Summer Goals

You set up a schedule at the beginning of the school year to manage all your activities. Why not approach summer the same way? The better you schedule, the more projects and activities you'll be able to take on, whether it's learning something new, going on an exciting trip, or getting to the bottom of that summer reading list.

Maximize your summer!

JOJO FACTS

....

- JoJo juggles dancing, singing, making YouTube videos, and working with huge companies like Nickelodeon and Walmart—and that's not even counting her schoolwork!

- JoJo has about a million goals, and she's determined to turn her dreams into realities.

Summertime doesn't have to be lazy time!

List your summer goals!

What do *you* want to achieve this summer? Goals and dreams are pretty personal, but here are a few ideas to help you get started.

Goal #1: Learn something new.
You learned to ice skate last winter. Why not learn to swim this summer? Already know how to swim? Amazing! You can take swimming to the next level by learning a new stroke, completing more laps across the pool, or treading water for a really long time.

Goal #2: Make new friends.
Siwanatorz are always on the lookout for new friends. Over the summer, we don't always get to spend time with our school friends. It's okay to miss them, but this is also a chance to make new friends. Maybe you're going to sleepaway camp for the first time and haven't met any of your bunkmates yet. Maybe you've moved to a new neighborhood and joined the community pool. Everyone you haven't met yet is a potential new friend!

Goal #3: Fight summer slide.
Have you ever heard of the term *summer slide?* That's what teachers call our forgetting lessons we learned during the school year over the summer. But you don't have to be a summer slider! Maybe your school assigns a summer reading list every year. Read every book you can! Maybe you can't quite remember a math lesson your teachers taught last spring. Grab your textbook and refresh your memory.

Goal #4: Leave time for spontaneity!
JoJo believes in mixing having a plan and being spontaneous. She can be random and silly and *still* have a plan for the next five years. And so can you! Having a list of goals and plans to achieve them doesn't mean you can't be silly from time to time (or almost all the time).

What are *your* goals this summer? List them here!

_____

_____

_____

_____

_____

_____

_____

_____

MESSAGES FROM JOJO

"I always have a plan."

"Random fun always has its place. (You're talking to the girl who dumps juice on her head, come on.)"

15

End-of-School Word Game

You already know how much JoJo loves to make her friends and family laugh. In honor of the end of school, here's a word game to make you and your friends laugh.

Without telling your friends anything about the story below, ask them to help you fill in the blanks with the type of words indicated below each blank—a name, a noun, a verb, and so on. Chances are, when you read back the story with the blanks filled in, it will be hilarious!

_____ was so excited for the last day of school. She was going to give
____girl's name____

her best friends _____ to commemorate the end of the year. She was
_____noun_____

sure they would love their gifts.

Next, she was going to spend the beginning of summer at _____.
_____place____

She'd never been there before, but she was excited to see it. While she was

there, she would try new things like _____ and _____, and she
_____verb_____ _____verb____

couldn't wait to taste _____. Maybe she would even learn how to cook
____type of food____

it herself!

Next, she was going to camp to master her _____. She was going to
_____activity____

learn _____, _____, and _____! By the time camp
____skill____ ____skill____ ____skill____

was over, she was sure she'd be winning every contest and starring in every

performance!

After camp, she was going to visit her _____. She couldn't wait! She
_____type of relative____

knew that together they would _____ and _____ and
_____verb_____ _____verb____

bake _____.
____type of food____

But she was also excited to get back home to her friends at the end of the summer. Before school started again, they would _____ and

_____ and definitely eat lots of _____. Before she knew it, it would be time for the school year to begin!

Summer

(June–August)

1

SUMMER WORD SCRAMBLE

It's summertime, and the weather is fine! Celebrate the sunshine with a few of our favorite summery words.

Can you unscramble these summer words?

BCHAE _____

MMSIWIGN _____

BRUUNS _____

THO _____

DEANOMLE _____

BBCUEEAR _____

Answers: beach, swimming, sunburn, hot, lemonade, barbecue

Try a new swimming stroke!

School's Out, But Keep Learning All Summer Long!

Learning doesn't have to be limited to the school day or even the school year! Summertime is the perfect time to take on a project of your own.

Perfect a new dance move!

Idea #1: Set a summer reading goal.

Some schools give kids a list of books to read over the summer. But whether your school does that or not, summer is a great time for reading! (Why else do you think they call books "beach reads"?!) Maybe there's a fantasy series you've been waiting to dig into. Or maybe you want to read a certain number of books each month. Or maybe you're finally ready to try your older sibling's favorite book. It's *your* reading goal, so anything goes.

Idea #2: Learn a new language.

This is a big one, and let's admit it, you're probably not going to master a new language all by yourself over the summer. But that's no reason not to get started! Maybe you like the sound of Italian words or there's a student in your class who moved to the United States from another country, and you want to surprise him or her by speaking in their native language. Whatever your reason, learning a new language is fun! You might find a website that offers lessons or a book with translations. Or maybe you have a family friend who's fluent and can give you lessons. Learning a new language is hard work, but it is definitely rewarding.

Idea #3: Expand your vocabulary.

Okay, we know this one sounds boring, but trust us, it's actually a lot of fun. Learning new words is a lot like learning a new language, if you think about it. Plus words are really interesting: Did you know that *defenestrate* means to throw something out of a window? And that the word

JOJO FACT

. . . .

- JoJo loves learning!

MESSAGE FROM JOJO

"Don't be scared of being smart! Sure, smart kids get a little hate sometimes, but don't listen to what the haters say!"

in French for window is *fenêtre*? See how the two words are linked? It's kind of like putting puzzle pieces together. Also, when the school year starts in September and your teachers hear you using words like *bellicose, vehement,* and *vociferous* (look them up!), they'll know you're a hard worker!

Idea #4: Choreograph a dance routine to your favorite song.
If you love to dance as much as JoJo does, then this may be the summer activity for you! This is a great activity to do with a friend. Maybe your best friend knows some moves that you have yet to learn, and vice versa. Give each other lessons! Pick a song and come up with a great dance. Create costumes. Invite family and friends over to watch you perform. You can even record your dance to share with friends online!

What are some additional summer goals you can think of? List them below!

_____

_____

_____

_____

_____

_____

_____

_____

_____

Quality time is the best time!

3

Celebrate Father's Day with Quality Time

Maybe you get to see your dad every day, or you don't live with him full-time, or there's someone else in your life who's like a dad to you. Father's Day is a great excuse to spend some quality time together, just the two of you.

Activities You and Your Dad Can Do Together

Idea #1: Cook a meal.
Maybe your dad loves to grill. Then today is the perfect time for him to show you how to do it! Or maybe you love to bake brownies. Then today is a great day to teach him your secret ingredient. Or maybe neither of you is much of a cook at all. Then use today to pick out a recipe that's new to both of you, and master it together. Cooking is a great way to spend time together, and when you're done, you have a treat to share with the whole family!

Idea #2: Take a hike.
Is there a park nearby that you've been wanting to explore? Maybe it's not nearby at all and you'll have to drive a long way to reach a super special hiking trail. Either way, you'll be exploring together.

Idea #3: Spend a day at the beach.
One of the great things about Father's Day is that it falls in June, which means it's the perfect time of year to spend the day at the beach. Maybe you and your dad can build a sand castle together, or maybe you'll bury him in sand, or maybe he can take you out into the water beyond the break of the waves! However you spend your day enjoying the sun, sand, and surf, it will be better because you spent it together.

Can you think of some other great ways to spend a day with your dad? Maybe the two of you can even brainstorm some ideas together!

_____

_____

_____

_____

_____

_____

_____

_____

_____

_____

_____

_____

_____

_____

_____

_____

JOJO FACTS

• JoJo says her dad is more like a friend than a parent!

• When JoJo and her dad are together, they make special plans to go out to lunch or dinner, just the two of them, or to spend a whole day together.

MESSAGE FROM JOJO

"My dad and me, we're two peas in a pod."

4

Plan a Fourth of July Bike Parade

Plan your very own parade for your neighborhood. All you need is your friends, your bikes, and a whole lot of red, white, and blue!

Tips to Plan Your Fourth of July Bike Parade

Tip #1: First, invite your friends to participate. Remember, the more decorated bikes, the more impressive your parade will look. So the more the merrier!

Fireworks! Barbecues! Parades!

Tip #2: Plan a route around your neighborhood, and pick a time for your parade to start. Then spread the word so your friends and neighbors can watch.

Tip #3: Invite your friends over to your house for a bike-decorating party. You'll need ribbons and streamers to decorate your handlebars and in between the spokes of your wheels. You can use colored paper or foam board to cut out stars. Just make sure you stick to the colors of the day—red, white, and blue!

Tip #4: Bring some music. Throw some portable speakers into your bike basket, and create a medley of patriotic songs like *America the Beautiful, The Star-Spangled Banner, God Bless America*, and more!

Tip #5: Don't just decorate your bikes. Dress up too! You and your friends can wear outfits in red, white, and blue. You can paint stars and stripes on your cheeks with face paint.

Tip #6: Finish with a backyard barbecue! Surprise your friends by having the parade route lead right to your backyard, with everything set up for a delicious Fourth of July celebration! Hot dogs, hamburgers, maybe even cupcakes decorated with red, white, and blue frosting. Happy Birthday, America!

Happy Birthday, America!

Aloha!

5

MAKE A HOMEMADE LEI

If springtime is for planting, then summertime is for blooming! But this year, do more with flowers than putting them in a vase. Make the most of summer blooms—*and* make a fashion statement—by creating your very own lei.

LEI FACT

....

- A lei is a necklace made out of flowers.

Make your own lei by following these steps!

Step #1: Gather some flowers. If you don't have flowers, you can use tissue-paper roses like the ones on page 68!

Step #2: Cut off the flower stems.

Step #3: Cut some string. (Bonus Tip: If you're using thread, cut double the length that you want your lei to be so that you can double it and make it sturdier.)

Step #4: Take a large needle and thread your string until it's doubled over, then tie the ends together to form a knot—this will keep your threaded flowers from falling off. Make sure you leave enough room so that you're able to tie the ends together when you're done.

Step #5: Very carefully, stick the needle into the center of your first flower.

Did you know the plural of "lei" is "lei"?

Step #6: Thread the rest of your flowers. If you're using different colored flowers, you can alternate colors or put the same colors next to each other to create chunks of color on your necklace. It's up to you, so be creative!

Step #7: Finish your lei by tying the ends of your string together. Slip your lei over your head, or give it as a gift!

In Hawaii, lei are presented to guests as they arrive or depart as a sign of affection.

6

Sneaker Decoration

Do you love sneakers? Create a pair worth showing off! Maybe you have an old pair lying around that still fits but doesn't quite show off your style or a plain white pair just waiting to be spruced up. You can even ask your parents to buy you a plain pair so you can decorate them! Either way, you're going to create a unique, one-of-a-kind pair that's totally you!

One of a kind!

How to Decorate Your Sneakers

Step #1: Start with sneakers.
Make sure you have your parents' permission before you get started, whether you're improving an old pair or starting from scratch with a plain pair.

Step #2: Paint and markers.
You can use fabric paint and markers to decorate your sneakers—paint a white pair a totally different color, create a collage of your favorite words, or even draw a hundred bows to show the world you're a Siwanator!

Step #3: Don't stop there.
You can use a glue gun to stick items to your sneakers. Maybe you have some old, inexpensive jewelry, like a broach or a pair of earrings, that would look amazing on the side of your shoes! You can even loop a necklace around the laces for some extra bling. (Just be careful not to pick something you don't want to lose. You never know when something might fall off!)

Step #4: How about buttons, sequins, and studs?
If your sneakers are made of a soft, thin fabric like canvas, you can probably use a needle and thread to sew accessories onto them. If the fabric is too thick or hard to pierce with a needle, use glue instead.

Unique!

Step #5: Did we mention glitter?
You can coat your sneakers with glue and then sprinkle them with glitter to create a pair of sparkly kicks!

Step #6: Take your new kicks out for a spin!
(This step is pretty self-explanatory.)

JOJO JAYDEN FACT

....

- JoJo's brother, Jayden, loves sneakers almost as much as JoJo loves bows!

Express yourself!

7

Set Up Camp in Your Backyard

Summertime is a great time for camping—
the weather is warm, it stays light out longer, and
there's no school to get up for in the morning. And
you don't have to go far to set up camp—try your
own backyard! You get to spend the night under the
stars, but you're still close to home (and to things
like bathrooms and refrigerators—and parents!). So
invite a few friends, your siblings, or even
your parents to join you for a very special—
and very convenient—camping trip.
Here are a few tips for setting up camp in your
very own backyard.

Ghost
stories!

Backyard Camping Tips

Tip #1: Pull out the sleeping bags.
Tents are great, but if it's warm and dry, ditch the tents and lay your sleeping bags on the lawn to sleep under the stars!

Tip #2: Tell scary stories.
No camping trip is complete without ghost stories. Take turns telling the scariest story you know. Or play a storytelling game! Here's how it works:
o Sit in a circle with your friends and family.
o Hold the flashlight and begin your story with an opening sentence. ("It was a dark and stormy night" is always a great start.)
o Pass the flashlight to the person sitting next to you, who can add the next sentence, and then pass the flashlight to the person sitting on their other side, who will add the one after.
o Keep going around the circle until it gets back to you—now, it's your job to give the story its big finish!

Tip #3: Make s'mores.
A camping trip isn't a camping trip until you make s'mores—delicious sandwiches of graham crackers, marshmallows, and chocolate. If your backyard has a fire pit, you're all set! (If not, you can make s'mores over the grill or even in the oven in a pinch—more on that below.) Find a stick (or even a chopstick from the kitchen—another advantage to being close to home!) and put a marshmallow on the end. Then hold the stick over the fire until your marshmallow is puffy and darkened. Finally, put a piece of chocolate on a graham cracker, and use another cracker to slide the marshmallow onto the chocolate. Use that same cracker to top off your "sandwich." Voilá! Some people like their marshmallows so well done that they turn black, and others like them toasty brown.

Bonus Tips:

Maybe you live in an apartment and you don't have a backyard—no problem! Set up camp in your living room. Spread out your sleeping bags, turn off the lights, and use flashlights instead. You can even make indoor s'mores in the oven! Here's how:

1: Heat the oven to 350 degrees.

2: Take a piece of tin foil and layer your ingredients on top: a graham cracker on the bottom, then a marshmallow (cut it in half if you need to make it stay put), chocolate, then another graham cracker on top.

3: Bake until the marshmallow is golden brown.

4: Let cool—then eat!

Summertime is a great time for camping!

Try Something New

There are so many different ways to try something new—whether it's learning a new lesson at school, playing a new sport, or tasting a new food. The key is not to be afraid to experience all the different things out there. How else will you learn what you like?

Tip #1: Try a new food.

Maybe the idea of raw fish grosses you out, so you've never tried sushi. Or maybe your parents are big on brussels sprouts, but you think they look downright weird. But how will you know what you like if you don't at least taste a little bit of everything? Think of tasting new foods as the easiest way to try something new. All you have to do is open your mouth! But you have every right to spit something out if you don't like it—after all, when it comes to food, whether or not you like something is literally a matter of taste.

Tip #2: It's not gonna be perfect.

Trust us on this one: Maybe you want to try out for the football team, and it turns out you can't throw the ball as far as the other kids. That's the thing about trying something new: Some things will come really easily to you, and other things won't. But that doesn't mean you shouldn't try them! If you really like something, all the hard work you have to put in to master it will be worth it—in fact, it won't feel like work at all.

Tip #3: But be honest.

Trying new things is great, but so is loving the things you love. So if you try something new and it turns out you don't love it, that's okay. Don't forget about JoJo and softball—in the end, she stopped playing to make more time for dancing, because dance was more important to her. Maybe your parents really want you to play the piano, but you prefer the violin. Or maybe your best friend is all about a new TV show, but you just don't get it. That's the thing about trying new things—it's how you discover what you really love.

Is there a food you've been putting off tasting? A dance routine that intimidates you? Make a list of five new things you

JOJO FACTS

- JoJo loves trying new things!

- Remember when JoJo took time away from dance to join the softball team? In the end, she had to give up softball to make more time for dance, but she made some great friends and learned some new skills along the way.

want to try this summer!

1. _____

2. _____

3. _____

4. _____

5. _____

MESSAGES FROM JOJO

"Remember that when a door closes, another door opens!"

"Starting over is all about the learning curve!"

9

Perfect Your Side Ponytail

Let's face it: Pulling, brushing, and smoothing
your hair into the perfect ponytail can be tricky.
But with these tried-and-true steps from JoJo,
you'll be rocking your ponytail in no time!

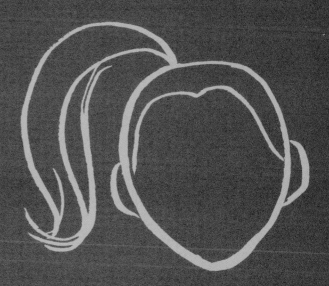

Let's make perfect ponytails!

Step #1: Brush all your hair onto the side of your head—you pick, left or right! It's a lot easier to make a ponytail when your hair is free of knots and tangles.

Step #2: Now it's time for hairspray. Spray it all over your hair to get the strands to stay in place.

Step #3: Brush some more! Slick all of your hair into place so there are no lumps or bumps.

Step #4: Ponytail holder time! JoJo actually uses four thick ponytail holders to keep her ponytail in place, but you can use whatever works best for you. Maybe you like a thick holder like JoJo, or maybe you prefer a thin elastic. There are no rules, so whatever works!

Bonus steps to take your ponytail to the next level!
Step #5: You can use more hairspray to get rid of any wispy, flyaway hairs.

Step #6: You can use a hot flat iron to make your ponytail sleek and smooth. (Or use a curling iron to curl it!)

Step #7: And of course, no JoJo ponytail is complete without a bow!

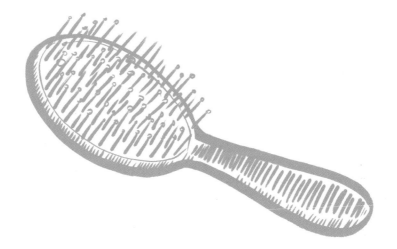

JOJO FACTS

- Side ponytails are JoJo's signature hairstyle!

- Ponytails are a great way to show off your newest bow!

- For more on making your very own bow, check out page 39.

MESSAGE FROM JOJO

"I wear the same exact four ponytail holders every day of my life: pink, yellow, orange, and lime green!"

10

JoJo Has Her Bow—Come Up With Your Own Signature Accessory!

Now that you've perfected your JoJo-style side ponytail, it's time to come up with a signature style all your own. Your signature accessory should tell the world something about you without saying a word.

Find something you love as much as JoJo loves her costumes!

Find your signature style.

Idea #1: A Headband

Trends come and go—sometimes headbands are in, sometimes they're out. But part of what makes a signature accessory so signature is that you don't care about what's fashionable. You only care about what you like to wear! (Actually, that's always a good philosophy.) So don't let trends cramp your style. If you feel great wearing a headband every day, then do it!

There's a reason it's called a signature accessory!

Idea #2: A Scarf

Scarves are great when it's cold outside, but did you know there are lightweight scarves for summertime too? A scarf can be a great way to add a bit of flair to your outfit—you can add a colorful scarf to a drab outfits and suddenly it's not as drab. Or you can tie a silky scarf around your neck to make a casual outfit look a whole lot fancier. Scarves are great because there are so many different kinds—wool scarves, silk scarves, cotton scarves, and more—and you can collect them in pretty much every color and pattern imaginable!

MESSAGE FROM JOJO

"I would have slept in my dance costume if I could!"

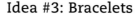

- JoJo was just a toddler when she danced her first solo. Her favorite part of the costume was the huge, orange, glittery bows that adorned her curly pigtails. She stuck with her bows, and soon they were her signature accessory.

Idea #3: Bracelets

Jewelry can make for a great signature accessory because it's easy to find a piece of jewelry that you can wear every day. Just remember, it's a signature accessory, so you want it to stand out! Maybe it's a stack of bracelets up one arm, or maybe a charm bracelet that you add to every year until it's jingling and jangling with charms that represent your favorite things.

Idea #4: A Hairstyle

Experiment with your hair to come up with your own signature hairstyle! Maybe you love how you look with bangs, or you always wear your hair in a French braid, or you have hair that's naturally curly and your curls are your signature. Just don't forget, signature accessories are personal. The key to a signature accessory or hairstyle is that it makes you feel comfortable—it makes you feel like *you*!

11

Cheer Someone On

A big part of being a Siwanator is supporting your friends and family. Sometimes it's your time to shine—when you're perfecting your dance moves or recording your latest song—but sometimes, there's nothing better than letting the people around you take center stage.

GO! GO! GO!

Be someone's biggest fan!

How can you show the people around you that you're rooting for them? Here are a few tips!

Tip #1: Show up.
Maybe your brother is on the local baseball team or your best friend has a swim meet coming up. We're all so busy these days, it can be hard to keep track of our friends' activities and achievements when we're caught up with our own. Make an effort to be there when you know a friend or family member has a big day.

Be a cheerleader!

Tip #2: Be a cheerleader.
When you do show up, be a fan. If you went to your favorite singer's concert, you wouldn't just sit there. You would be on your feet, dancing to the music, singing along, and cheering and applauding, right? So do the same for your friends and family!

Tip #3: Pay attention.
Sometimes the big moments aren't as easy to recognize as sporting events and performances. Maybe your big sister has a scary doctor's appointment or your mom is interviewing for a new job. Just because you can't show up at tests and interviews to cheer your family on doesn't mean you can't support them. Maybe leave a good-luck note in your sister's backpack the morning of her big test or give your mom a special hug to let her know you'll be rooting for her.

Tip #4: Just be there.

Another way to be a fan is to let the people you love know that you'll be there for them no matter what. It's not just about cheering each other on for the big events—sometimes our friends and family need a reminder that they've got a fan for no reason at all. Let the people you love know that you're rooting for them.

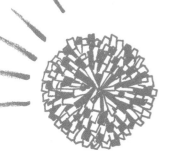

JOJO FACTS

- JoJo's brother, Jayden, loves playing baseball, and whenever JoJo is back in Omaha, her favorite thing to do (besides hanging out with her friends!) is watching her brother play baseball.

- Just because JoJo is a star doesn't mean she isn't a fan too—in fact, she tries to be Jayden's *biggest* fan.

MESSAGES FROM JOJO

"Jayden's so talented, and I love going to his games and taking a million pictures!"

"Part of being a family is being there for each other—
so support the people you love."

Why did the chicken cross the road?

12

Make Up Your Own Joke

Being funny is a great way to break the ice when you meet new people or to make an awkward moment feel less awkward. Here are a few tried-and-true tips for being funny—just like JoJo!

JoJo's Tips for Being Funny

Tip #1: Come up with your own punch line to the classics.

We've all heard the jokes that begin with, "Knock, knock. Who's there?" Or "Why did the chicken cross the road?" A great way to make people laugh it to surprise them! Set up the beginning of a familiar joke, but then change the end of the joke with your very own punch line!

Tip #2: Have a running joke.

JoJo has an ongoing joke with her dad involving fart spray. Why not have a running joke of your own? Maybe you and your best friend have a crush on the same movie star, and you pass each other pictures of him onto which you've written thought bubbles and phrases. The great thing about jokes like these is that they're not just funny—they're also like a secret you get to share with someone else.

Tip #3: Laugh at yourself.

We've all experienced some embarrassing moment. Maybe we tripped during a performance or walked out of the bathroom with toilet paper stuck to our sneakers. These moments can be mortifying, but they can also be hilarious! Try to get over your embarrassment and have some fun instead. It's important not to take yourself too seriously—you'll miss out on a lot of fun if you do.

JOJO FACTS

....

- JoJo loves a good joke.

- JoJo and her dad have a prank tradition involving fart spray and battling to see who can come up with the most creative way to use it. (So far, JoJo's winning, of course!)

Knock, knock.

Who's there?

177

Tip #4: When all else fails, wear a funny costume.
You already know how much JoJo loves dressing up. But sometimes the best costume doesn't involve bows and sequins for your latest dance performance. A costume can also be a great way to make people laugh without saying a word! Dress up as a hot dog or a sandwich, or dress up like your mom, your dad, or your best friend.

MESSAGE FROM JOJO

"You never know when you might need to lighten the mood with a joke!"

13

Troll Someone on Social Media—in a Good Way

Social media can be pretty powerful. It's a wonderful way for JoJo to express herself and connect with her fans—and the people she's fangirling too. Unfortunately, we all know that some people don't spend their time on social media connecting in a positive way, like JoJo does. Some people log on to spread negativity—whether they're trashing a celebrity, a classmate, or even a (former) friend. Let's work together to make social media a place that celebrates kindness and ignores the bullies.

Ways to Be a Positive Troll on Social Media

Step #1: First, make sure you have your parents' permission to post messages online. It might sound lame, but plenty of parents are worried about our online presence—and with all the bullies out there, we don't blame them! Talk to your parents about why you want to express yourself online, and listen when they express their concerns.

Step #2: Post a positive message on someone's social media. Tell a friend how much you love her picture on Instagram, or make a positive comment on her latest video. It's guaranteed to make her day!

Step #3: Create a positive post on your account. Maybe it's a picture of you and your best friend with a caption about what makes your friendship so special or a Snapchat in which you tell the world how awesome your parents are. Every time you post to social media, think of it as a chance to put some positivity out into the world.

Step #4: Be a fan, whether it's posting a positive review of a book you loved, commenting on your favorite singer's latest video, or letting your favorite team know you've got their back. Even celebrities love to hear from their fans on social media, so let them know that you're one of their biggest fans. You might even get a message back!

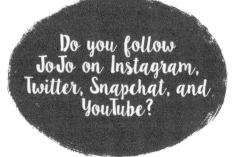

Do you follow JoJo on Instagram, Twitter, Snapchat, and YouTube?

JOJO FACT

- When JoJo faced haters on social media for the first time, she turned to her mom for support, and Jessalynn reminded her that what matters is how you feel about yourself.

MESSAGE FROM JOJO

"Everyone has the potential to make the world a better place if they're kind."

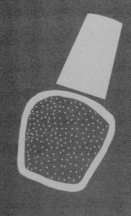

14

Have a Luxurious Mother/ Daughter Spa Day

What do you like to do with your mom? Did you know you can have a glamorous spa day together without ever leaving the house?

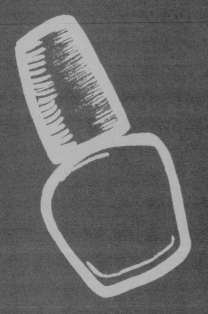

Relaaaax!

Tips for the Perfect Spa Day

Tip #1: Make your own body scrub.
Mix brown sugar with coconut oil for a yummy-smelling body scrub, under your mom's supervision. The oil can get messy, so make sure to do this in your bathroom. Rub the homemade scrub on your feet, legs, and arms, then wash it off. Voila! You'll have softer, smoother skin.

Hint: Add a drop of vanilla or peppermint extract or even cocoa powder to the mix to personalize it with your favorite scent!

Tip #2: Take turns giving each other pedicures.
Soak your clean, polish-free feet in warm water in the bathtub or a large basin for five minutes. (Have Mom check the temp!) Sip lemon-infused water while you wait. (Squeeze one lemon wedge into a glass of water.) Then scrub your feet with your homemade body scrub. Rinse, and use a soothing lotion on top. Add cuticle oil (olive oil or coconut oil works just as well) to your nails. Finish with two coats of nail polish and a clear topcoat for beautiful, summer-worthy toes!

Tip #3: Finish with a face mask yummy enough to eat!
Did you know yogurt is great for your skin? You and your mom can make face masks by blending a single serving of Greek yogurt with a drizzle of honey and the juice from half a lemon. Mix it all up, put it in the freezer until it's chilled, apply it to clean skin, and let it sit for ten minutes. When you're done, rinse it off with warm water. Avoid the eye area, but if the yogurt sneaks into your mouth, that's okay. Ask Mom to apply your mask for you, if you need help.

Spa—aaaaah!

JOJO FACTS

....

- JoJo and her mom, Jessalynn, are best friends.

- JoJo is a total homebody!

Bonus Tips:
- Wear comfy loungewear, like pajamas or a soft robe.
- Pick out fun magazines or a TV show in advance—you'll want something fun to do while you're soaking your feet or waiting for your face mask to set!
- Use supplies you already own, and get creative—brown sugar can be swapped out for white sugar, and oatmeal can be swapped for Greek yogurt.
- Use soft headbands to keep your hair back during your spa treatments.
- Relax and have fun!

184

> *Nothing says summertime quite like ice cream.*

15

Treat Your Friends to an Ice Cream Sundae Buffet!

Is there anything better than ice cream in the summertime? However you decide to spend the dog days of summer—lounging by the pool, crashing through ocean waves, playing a round of beach volleyball—we can all agree that an ice cream treat is an excellent way to end your day. We can think of one way to make that ice cream treat even better—sharing it with your friends, of course!

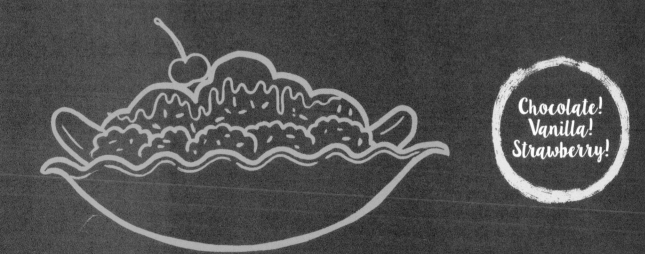

> *Chocolate! Vanilla! Strawberry!*

Tips for Creating the World's Greatest Ice Cream Sundae Buffet

Invite your friends over for an ice cream party. Line up these ingredients—on the kitchen counter, on the dining room table, or in your backyard—with spoons and scoopers so that your friends can help themselves! (Just make sure Mom and Dad are okay with the mess.) This way, everyone will be able to create their own perfect version of an ice cream sundae. Here's what you'll need:

1. Ice cream
Vanilla may be the traditional ice cream sundae flavor—and there's nothing wrong with being classic!—but offer your friends a little more variety. Have cartons of chocolate and strawberry, vanilla fudge and coffee. Get exotic with flavors like dulce de leche and chocolate chip cookie dough!

2. Sauce
We all love a good hot fudge sundae, but don't stop there. Offer caramel sauce and strawberry sauce. Be creative—offer marshmallow fluff and peanut butter.

3. Toppings
Just a few suggestions to help you get started: Whipped cream, crushed-up cookies, cut-up bananas and strawberries, chocolate chips, peanut butter chips, cookie dough, raisins, and nuts.

4. Sprinkles
You didn't think we forgot about sprinkles, did you? Offer the prettiest, brightest, and "rainbowiest" sprinkles you can find!

Second helpings!

5. And a cherry on top

This is optional, but the classic ice cream sundae is adorned with a cherry on top. Leave a bowl of cherries (make sure they're free of pits!) at the end of your buffet so that your guests can add the finishing touch to their sundaes.

Enough sprinkles to make every bite more colorful than the last!

Toppings— lots of toppings!